My Kind of People

My Kind of People

by
Mike Murphy

Butternut Press, Westport, Ontario

Canadian Cataloguing in Publication Data
Murphy, Mike, 1927 –
My kind of people
ISBN 0-921575-02-5

1. Murphy, Mike, 1927 –   .   2. Ontario – History – 1918-1945.*
3. Ontario – History – 1945 –   .*   4. Ontario – Biography.   I. Title.
FC3076.1.M8A3 1987   971.3'04'0924   C87-094856-3
F1058.M8A3 1987

Printed and bound in Canada

Butternut Press Inc.
P.O. Box 166, Westport
Ontario, K0G 1X0

Editor: *Pamela Fry*
Designer: *Marjory Dennis*
Cover Illustration: *Florence Mansfield*

Contents

To my brother, Pete

Author's Acknowledgements

I have dedicated this book to my brother, Pete, who was not always happy with the life-style my friends and I chose, but loved us just the same.

I also want to dedicate it to my friends themselves – especially those wonderful people in the Kingston area. After the death of my brother they did so much to ease the pain of losing him. Included in my list of life-time companions who deserve special mention are "Big" Joe Fahey and his brother Jack; "Little" Pete Murphy, Frank Spence, Cecil Kenney; and my three first cousins, Margaret, Rosie, and Lucy.

Among my Toronto friends, I especially want to mention Garfield Franklin Montgomery ("Loophole"), Dave Coon, Bruce McLean, George Yemec, and a couple of gals named Cheryl and Michel.

Lastly, I would like to pay homage to all my old Jesuit teachers, who taught a boy early how to survive the pitfalls of life; and to my editor, Pam Fry.

Mike Murphy, Toronto. 1987

My kind of people 1

How I Got Started

Many years ago on hot summer nights in the village of Elgin, my Aunt, Mary Anne, used to sit on the verandah, partly hidden by climbing green ivy, waiting for the evening breeze.

My brother and I would lie lazily in the petunia-framed grass, dodging the zooming bats which were always part of those summer nights.

Our big, rambling frame house was across from the Empire Hotel, one of the few human watering-holes along the Rideau chain of lakes between Kingston and Ottawa.

I should explain how it was we were living with my aunt Mary Anne, and her two sisters, all of them retired schoolteachers. Me and my brother, Pete, had been born a year apart. So I arrived on this planet in 1927. We were living in Kingston at the time, and my father was a marine engineer. After Pete and I had turned eight and nine, my mother died giving birth to twins. There was no way my father could take us on, so we were packed off to Elgin, where we spent the next seven years. Looking back, it was a pretty good sort of life we had there, full of fun, surprises, and a couple of mysteries.

One of the continuing mysteries was my Aunt Mary Anne's age. I don't think a day ever passed when one of the village children would not ask her how old she was. Her answer was always the same, "Can you keep a secret?" If the child nodded or answered "Yes," she would then reply, "So can I."

She kept many secrets, as she sat on that verandah reading the daily paper or the *Saturday Evening Post*. Some of her special secrets she shared with me.

The stillness of the village was broken only by the comings and goings of the district regulars and visiting American tourists.

It was the American visitors who gave a child, born to wonder, his first glimpse of the outside world.

They were different. They talked differently, looked different, dressed differently, and, I suppose, just plain acted differently.

In most instances when a child wonders, the wonder dies sooner than the daffodils. Yet my enchantment with some of these people has lasted a lifetime.

Many of the visitors had made it big in the worldly sense. There was a famous actor, a Hockey Hall of Famer, a boxer who had gone the distance and lost the heavyweight championship by a decision.

There were many renowned professionals, judges, doctors, a famous New York District Attorney, and the head of the largest newsgathering service in the world.

You could fill a couple of pages in the *Who's Who* with their names.

With all my wondering, which was gradually giving me a much deeper awareness of life and a keener relish for the outside world, I could not comprehend what brought these people here.

It took years and years of living to realize that everything important begins with wonder.

Yet it took even longer to realize that learning, great art, and success stand on the acknowledgement that they are not really *the* important things in life.

The important things are already there for us all to enjoy and share ... the lakes, the sun, the fresh air, the laughter, love, and our daily encounters with each other.

A day never passed in the village that I was not made aware of this – but I wasn't always listening.

I remember old Ab Mattice, the bartender, pushing his wheelbarrow around the visiting cars on his way to the icehouse. He would stop in front of our house, one of the leisurely pauses he always made when he walked more than half a block.

On one particular day he stopped and said to me, "Gawd boy, ain't it funny. These tourists is all the same. They work their asses off in those big Americans cities to save enough to come here and spend it!"

Moving another few feet, he stopped again and after letting go a big gob of tobacco juice, proclaimed, "Well, I already got what they're saving for, so the only thing I save is myself."

On his return from these short trips, which seemed to take so much out of him, he would not go directly to the hotel. Instead, he would park the barrow beside the outhouse and disappear for a spell.

Although he always prided himself on not taking a drink on the job, he kept a bottle hidden under his private toilet paper, the Eaton's catalogue. Like a more modern-day philosopher's statement regarding the nation's bedrooms, old Ab had a thing about the nation not having any business in his rest-room.

Speaking of outhouses, everybody had one in those days. The man you called when you wanted it cleaned was Jack Pope, or "the Protestant Pope" as he was known in the village. I once asked Jack, while holding my nose, how he liked his job. "Not bad," he said. "The money is good, fifty cents a hole; and if you get a six-holer like up at the school, you can make a couple of day's pay in no time. The only thing, most people have to be sitting right in it before they give me a call."

Another character I remember in Elgin was old Sailor Rankin. He used to park in front of our house when he visited the hotel, and when he returned a couple of hours later, he would look up to the verandah through his thick glasses and say, "Good evening, Miss Murphy." Little did he know that Mary Anne would disappear into the house the moment she saw him leave the hotel. She was pretty well set against drinking, but that was mainly because of my grandmother. Uncle Willie, too, for that matter, but maybe I'd better tell you a bit about both of them.

Grandmother Hannah was my father's mother. She was pretty old when I first laid eyes on her, and older still when she died at ninety-three. My grandfather, Peter Murphy, had also been a marine engineer. She married him in Kingston and they settled there for a couple of years. However, Hannah had a high opinion of herself, and it wasn't long before she decided it was below her dignity to be married to a sailor, so she talked him into buying a farm, three miles from Elgin, on Delta Lake. She chose the setting herself, because across the lake, in the village of Delta, there once dwelt her favourite poet.

His name was Frederick Wright, and he was born in Dublin, Ireland, on November 14, 1810. At the age of twenty-two, he graduated from Trinity College and emigrated to Canada a year later. He first settled in Kemptville, where he married in 1836. In 1853, he moved to Delta, and here he was to pen many of his famous poems. These included a volume entitled, *Wayside Pencillings*. In 1864, he came up with another volume of gems: *The Lays of a Pilgrim*.

Now before you get the idea that the lays of this pilgrim referred to the number of pilgrims he managed to lay, I want to put you straight. His poems were all of a religious nature. He was evidently suffering a little remorse for what he considered to have been a sinful life, but he always seemed to have hope that he would be granted a happy hereafter.

One needs to only look at some of the titles to realize that they were not poems concerning lust: ... 'My Pilgrimage is Soon Over," "I am Weary of Earth," and "My Heart is Sad." Like Gram, he soon found the Delta area wasn't all that it had been cracked up to be. One of the poems she liked to read over and over to my brother and me was titled "This is Not a Joyous Spot."

Unfortunately, Freddy didn't manage to get out of Delta until late in life. He moved to the village of Westport in 1867, and died there nine years later. Under more favourable auspices, and given more leisure for literary pursuits, "The Pilgrim Poet" would have un-doubtedly stamped his name permanently upon the literature of Canada.

So that all may bear witness to some of Hannah's favourites, I will quote a few lines from a poem written by Freddy to his friend, Helen Rich:

> *As time moves on its steady race,*
> *More solemn scenes unfold,*
> *The bended form and sober face*
> *Show we are growing old.*

On her better days, Gram used to like poems in a lighter vein, such as the one penned by Tim Soper, a lesser-known poet in that area. Timothy, it seems, had taken a bag of oats to Merrickville to be ground for his neighbour, Tommy O'Connor. On his return he left the bag beside the road, just by the long lane that wound its way to the O'Connor house. So that nobody who came along would mistake the owner of the grist, he pinned the following poem to the bag:

> *Here I lie upon my back,*
> *My name is an Irish sack,*
> *Touch me not, upon your honour,*
> *For I belong to Tommy Connor.*

Getting back to Hannah, you can now see she was far too cultured to be either a sailor's or a farmer's wife. But I want you to know there must have been quite a bit of romance going between herself and her husband. She was to bear nine children. After the last child entered the world, she felt she had contributed quite enough. From then on, she refused to do even the most menial task around the house. Grandfather waited on her hand and foot until he became an invalid, and was confined to bed for the last ten years of his life.

By this time, the family had all grown up, but the girls learned early that they were to be their mother's servants for the rest of their lives. Two of them, Kate and Tess, finally escaped when they got married. But the other three, Lucy, Mary Anne, and Helena, never did. After the death of Grandad, the three of them left the farm and purchased a home in Elgin, taking Gram with them.

When Pete and I moved into that house, our room was next to Gram's, and we got to see her quite often. She seldom left her own room, and then only came to the head of the stairs, where she would shout down an order to one of our aunts. But early each morning, she would wake my brother and me with the same words: "Rise and shine you wee ones."

She was always dressed in a long, black gown that trailed three feet behind her. She also had a woollen cape slung over her shoulders and a long, wooden rosary hung around her neck, and reaching below her waist. The kind those cloistered monks always seem to be wearing.

Now it is my belief that this rosary was nothing more than an ornament or, at best, a symbol. To show she was no damn Protestant.

But she did insist on certain religious observances. Around our house, it was a nightly ritual, when the dishes had been washed and dried and put away, that everybody would go to Gram's room to say the evening prayers. As soon as she heard us coming, Gram would jump into the bed, and it was then that you could see the long, knee-length leather boots, laced to the top, disappearing beneath the blankets. Once safely in her nest, she would start moaning.

Sometimes the moans got so loud they would drown out the Hail Marys, but my Aunt Mary Anne, who led the prayers, always managed to get through five decades of the rosary, along with a string of other prayers. These sessions seemed to have a healing effect on Grandmother, however, for as soon as they were over she would appear from beneath the blankets, sit bolt upright, and demand a shot of brandy. I am not sure how many shots she needed to get through other trying episodes of the day, but you can take it there must have been quite a few – because she always smelled of booze. When the brandy ran out, as it often did during the prohibition days, there was hell to pay around the house. She finally solved the problem herself after she read an ad in the Brockville paper. It stated that you could have fortified bottles, containing beef, iron, and wine, shipped right to Elgin station at a reduced price, if ordered by the case. I take it that this mixture must have been a lot like bitters – still quite a popular drink around some circles today.

I think I would be safe in saying that a few private prayers must have been said for Hannah, as her daughters certainly knew she was a bit addicted to booze. But in that long list of people we prayed for in her room, her name was never brought up. However, her favourite son, Willie, did receive honourable mention. Willie was a dancer of note, played the fiddle, and could kick as high as a ten-foot ceiling. Gram's observation was that he was more Jordan than Murphy, which pleased her, since she never had much use for the Murphys. During her morning visits to Pete and me she would tell us that our Grandfather, Peter, was a fine man, but the Murphys as a whole were not too well thought of, even in Ireland. What Gramma did *not* mention, during her praises of Willie was that he, too, was quite a drinker. So much so that his sisters not only prayed for him, they decided to go one step further and ask for a miracle.

They were finally able to talk Willie into going on a trip to Brother André's Shrine in Montreal. So, when the day came, Mary Anne,

Lucy, and Willie boarded the train in Brockville, and headed east toward Montreal. Once it had pulled out of the station Willie excused himself. It seems he had smuggled a bottle aboard and did not want to drink in front of his benefactors. Well, ten minutes went by, and then half-an-hour. The girls began to get worried and hailed the conductor. The train was searched from top to bottom, but there was no sign of Uncle Will.

At last the train pulled into Cornwall, where the conductor notified the station agent and he, in turn, got hold of the section foreman. The foreman climbed onto a hand-car and putted back along the track. Twenty minutes later the hand-car and the foreman returned with a smiling passenger, Uncle Willie, who had already been making his way back on foot.

Mary Anne and Lucy decided then and there that two miracles in one day was too much to ask, so they stayed in Cornwall and took the next train home. They said that there was nary a scratch on Willie, and I have often wondered if he was ever included in all those miracles attributed to Brother André.

Then there was another Murphy we often prayed for. He was a distant cousin named Timmy. Timmy, according to Gram, was a good enough fellow, considering he was a Murphy. In fact she once stated that he was one of the finest who ever lived, but somehow had picked up a bad name around the community. He had married a Protestant, "Evil" Edith. According to Gram, she was the cause of all of his trouble, and the only good thing that could be said about her was she was a looker. Most of the community agreed, however, that Timmy was a poor provider, who drank too much and ran around. This according the Gramma, was pure hogwash. She claimed that any shortcomings the poor fellow had could be attributed to his wife.

Anyhow, it seems that, on Black Friday, Timmy was drowned in Lake Superior, when his ship went down and only two strong swimmers survived. His body was shipped home to Delta where he was waked. Few thought that Edith, who had left him three years previously, would show – but she did.

The last night of the wake, three of his old friends from Elgin decided to go over to Delta and pay their respects. The group included a fellow by the name of Churchill, another by the name of Coon, and the third, a fellow called Joe O'Meara. Before leaving on the six-mile trip by horse and cutter, they visited the Fahey hotel in Elgin and drank a few toasts to the departed. When they reached the wake house, they were a little late in arriving and there was only one person guarding the coffin – a very pretty woman. Now O'Meara's main claim to fame was that he always knew everybody on sight, but on this occasion his memory failed him. Walking up to the solitary mourner, and taking her hand by way of greeting, he said "How's your husband?" Looking kind of startled, she replied, "Rather peaceful for a change. Go over to the coffin and see for yourself."

Well, the three of them walked over, rather sheepishly and O'Meara, being the only Catholic, knelt down to say a little prayer. He had no more than begun when Coon, who was standing close by, tapped him on the shoulder and said, "I think your prayers have been answered, Joe. I could swear Tommy's eyelids are moving." That startled O'Meara alright, and he got up kind of quickly. He took a second look at the coffin and then back at Coon. "I think you could be right," he says. So they both stand there, a bit uncertain, because all those drinks had made their own eyesight a bit fuzzy. "Do you think I should go over and tell his wife?" says O'Meara to Coon. "It might be a good idea to mention it," replies Coon. "Churchill and I will wait outside."

So off he goes, and O'Meara heads over to break the news to Edith. However, when he faces the poor woman, he is kind of lost for words, so he mutters, "Timmy never looked better, you would swear he was alive and just sleeping." Well, if he had been startled by what he imagined he saw in the coffin, he was even more surprised by Edith's answer. "Dead or alive," she stated, "He is going out of here at nine in the morning for a funeral mass and burial in Philipsville cemetery." Dumbfounded as he was, O'Meara still tried to make a bit more small-talk before leaving. "It's lucky for you that he had a little insurance." Without batting an eye, Edith replied, "It's lucky for me he couldn't swim."

So it was that many of our evening prayers were not only for the living, but also for a few deceased, such as Timmy, whom my aunts felt might need them. During the winter months my father would be at home and sometimes, to break the monotony, he would add a few other names to the list. One that always brought Gram's head from beneath the covers was that of Dr. Peter Schofield, who had gained fame by delivering the first temperance address heard in Canada. The good Doctor was said to be a physician of the highest character, and a gentleman with the most scrupulous regard for the truth.

The following is what he was reported to have said in his address: "It is well authenticated that many habitual drinkers of ardent spirits are brought to their end by what it called SPONTANEOUS COMBUSTION. This occurs when a person takes fire and burns without any external application. One such event happened before my own eyes. It was the case of a young fellow about twenty-five years old. He had been a habitual drinker for many years. I was talking on the road to the owner of a blacksmith's shop, when all of a sudden we saw a bright light within his store. We thought the whole building was about to be engulfed in flames and ran toward it with the greatest precipitancy. On flinging open the door, we discovered the man standing erect in the midst of a widely-extended, silver-coloured blaze, bearing exactly the appearance of the wick of a candle in the midst of its own flame. The blacksmith seized the victim by the shoulder and jerked him to the door, upon which the flame was instantly extinguished. There was no other fire in the shop, so there was no possibility of fire having reached him from an external source. It was a pure case of SPONTANEOUS COMBUSTION! In his last moments, the poor fellow cried out that he knew he was now on the threshold of hell – and with those words, he gave up the ghost."

Speaking of ghosts, it was Gram's contention that they were always in our midst, especially at night, after the clock struck twelve. On many such an occasion, my brother and I would lie listening, as she conversed with somebody, we never knew whom.

She would begin her visits with these mysterious visitors with the words: "Be thou a spirit of earth or a goblin damned, bring with you air from heaven or blasts from hell?" We were later to learn that this greeting was borrowed from Shakespeare's *Hamlet*.

I take it that most of her visitors were from heaven, as she never mentioned having any acquaintances from down under. So the ghosts she spoke of were what she referred to as GOOD GHOSTS. They were usually deceased friends or neighbours, who returned to do some unfulfilled good works they had neglected while in the land of the living.

Some of her tales were not happenings she had witnessed personally, but she swore they were true, even though they had happened in Ireland years ago.

One story she often told was about an old priest in Dublin, who used to come back to the land of the living and say mass in a little church over there. It seems that the Man of God had a bad memory, and had neglected certain paid masses, even after receiving his stipend here on earth.

So it came as sort of a surprise when one morning she told us about a similar incident locally, regarding a priest who came back to have a mass said in the little hamlet of Ballycanoe. Unlike her Irish apparitions, this particular priest did not say the mass himself, but appeared and asked that the present pastor of the parish do the honours.

Nobody today seems to have ever heard of Ballycanoe, or of the other name it went by in my day, "Trevelyan." So just in case you might wish to visit the site of this ghostly story, I will give you directions.

You drive to the village of Athens and, near its centre, you take the county road south toward Mallorytown, some seven miles. You will then come to a fork in the road, and a battered old sign that once spelt "Trevelyan." Turning to your right, you follow this road some two miles and you will come to an abandoned old Catholic church, St. James the Less.

As you stand at its entrance and look to your left, you will see a lonely tombstone, standing just four feet from the walls of the church. The stone marks the grave of one of the most saintly priests to ever serve in the Diocese of Kingston. It is rather plain, some five feet high, with a cross at the top. The only words inscribed upon it, are his name, Father Joseph John Kelly, and the years he served in the church. He died in 1897.

The good works of Father Kelly have been well documented in the district, and his kindness to the poor will never be forgotten. I gather he was the type of person who even the departed would not mind calling on for a little favour.

Anyhow, after his death, his successor, Father J.J. Collins, was sitting in the rectory office, reading his breviary, when the old safe in the corner started to shake. I suppose when a three-hundred-pound vault starts doing a war dance in a room it does make one a little suspicious. The priest passed it off as just another mystery of life till one night, Father Kelly's sister Kate, who was keeping house for the new priest, came running in from the church. She was close to hysterics.

She told Collins that she had been praying in the church when her brother, that departed priest of the parish, appeared. To put it bluntly, he scared hell out of Katy, so she ran home as fast as she could. After hearing her out, Father Collins told her she should go back to the church and ask Father Kelly what he had on his mind. Although she was still terrified, Katy returned to the church and the dead priest appeared once more. She inquired what he wanted and he told her there were numerous paid masses that he had neglected. He said a list of these masses, and the stipends to cover them, would be found in the safe in the rectory office. He emphasized that he could only rest in peace in heaven after these masses had been said.

Katy returned, and gave Father Collins this information. Sure enough, when the priest followed her directions, an envelope with the necessary names and money was found. The masses were duly said, and Father Kelly was never heard from again.

Well, Gram may have dressed and looked like a witch, but to the best of my knowledge she never came back after she departed this planet. I guess like her poet friend she was weary of earth. I might also add she died a natural death; "old age," according to Doc Coon, and not spontaneous combustion.

Anyway, to get back to Elgin and my Aunt Mary Anne, one night I followed her as she hurried into the house to avoid Mr. Rankin and his drinking problem. "You know," I began, "I think Mr. Rankin is right when he says Mrs. Pinkerton hates everything small that walks on two feet or four," (I should explain that Mrs. Pinkerton was our next-door neighbour. She was one of those women who wanted everything just so about her house and garden. All the local kids were afraid of her, and so were the cats and dogs, because she was forever shooing us away.) Well, after I'd repeated what Mr. Rankin had said, my Aunt looked at me for what seemed like an hour. Finally she said, "Do you know what Mrs. Pinkerton told me just the other day? She said, 'Mickey'" – Mrs. Pinkerton and my Dad were the only ones who called me Mickey – "'is the kindest child I ever saw. Just the other day, when you gave him a nickel for a cone, he brought the cone over and gave it to me while I was ironing in the hot kitchen.'"

All at once I experienced a funny feeling.

I grabbed Mary Anne by the hand and looking up said, "Do you know what Mr. Rankin said about you! He said, 'That Miss Murphy is a saint, the way she dresses those two little boys and looks after them.'" As she turned her back and walked away I was wondering if she was experiencing the same feeling as I was.

I do know that the next day I let my two cats, Tom and Tiger, that I had kept hidden in the barn, out to play and frolic in the outdoors. They came and went as they pleased, *never* to be locked up again. Because by then I knew that even though Mrs. Pinkerton was a mite too fussy, she didn't really hate either children or animals.

I do know, too, that the next time Mr. Rankin said "Good night to you, Miss Murphy," Mary Anne was sitting on the verandah to reply, "Good night to you, Mr. Rankin. It's a lovely evening."

Yes, I was experiencing the important things in daily life, the love, the laughter and, I hope, a little humility.

Although I thought at the time that most of the laughter was part of the secrets shared by Mary Anne and me, I know now they were common knowledge.

Everybody knew that old Doc Mackie, who brought many a district child into the world, could chew tobacco and drink beer at the same time. The only time he needed to spit, it seemed, was when he was in the car. The bad part of that was that most times he forgot to roll down the window.

They also knew that Murray Stevens, the bait-man, had gone wrong in rearing his only son, a cub bear. When Murray stayed in the hotel too long, the bear, who waited in his truck, would grow restless. As a result, he would get out and climb an elm tree beside our house. The only way to get him down was to stand by the trunk at the bottom with an open pint of beer.

They also knew that the travelling music teacher, Daddy Thrasher, used to have to ply his larynx with a little alcohol, before coming to the various schools to teach the children how to hold a high c.

And they knew that you seldom heard a curse word outside that little hotel. The Bay Boys saw to that.

There were three of them: father George, a renowned skiff builder from Alexandria Bay, New York, and his two sons, Les and Ben. They would announce their arrival at the hotel rather boisterously with the words, "Perhaps you don't know who we be." Then, after a pause, they would answer their own question, "We're known far and wide as the Bay Boys." Yet, when they left, regardless of what shape they were in, old George would warn all present, "Watch your language when you get out on the street. Lady Murphy will be sitting on the verandah."

Ben, the most jovial of the three, would wave out at my brother and me with the greeting, "All the boys from Elgin call me Uncle Ben."

We children, growing up in the little hamlet, had many Uncle Bens – kind, lovable characters untouched by sophistication. Some of the pleasures they gave us as children swim back to my attention even now, and give me an extra tinge of pleasure. They were the kind of men who *made* life worth living, not the kind who *found* it that way.

Perhaps, as children, we laughed at their simplicity. Yet with the dawn of maturity, we came to realize that sophistication can dull a man's perception.

A day never passed that Mary Anne would not bring to my attention the kindness and accomplishments, however small, of these village people. Daily she stressed that you measure ordinary people not by what they do, but by how well they do it. She would point to the clean, white sheets blowing lazily in the wind on the hotel clothesline and say, "That is Mrs. Carr's showplace." Mrs. Carr was a domestic who did the laundry at the hotel, labouring daily to clothe and feed her son Billy.

Mary Anne would admire our staircase, built by the Bay Boys, a work of art like their skiffs, a few of which still ply the Rideau lakes.

She would call me to the window to watch Jack Pope digging the straightest, most exacting trench, unsurpassed even now by modern machinery. Each shovelful of dirt looked as if it had been precisely placed along its edge.

Many a night she called me from my warm bed to go with Doc

Feeney on sick call to some desolate farmhouse, miles away. I suppose I was about ten when I witnessed my first birth, and came to realize that it wasn't the stork that delivered babies – it was the good doctor. My job, when I went along to help him, was to fill a copper basin with water, place it on the wood stove, and give Doc a call when it started to boil. Driving home after one of these trips of mercy, I asked Doc if he ever got paid. He looked at me kind of funny-like and answered, "I always get paid by these poor people. Not in money, mind you, for money only buys that which is for sale."

Social Life in Elgin – and
I Meet the King

My closest friend, when I was growing up in the village of Elgin, was a fellow named Bill Franklin. The two of us never missed a social event, although we were both kept extremely busy attending school, and we both also had part-time jobs. There were many around the village who thought we kept a bit too busy, and they blamed us for a lot of little things that seemed to pop up.

There was the time that the local Provincial policeman ran out of gas on his motorcycle, while chasing a fugitive. It seems that Constable Butcher had to push his machine two miles back to the village, cursing all the way, remembering how he had just filled the gas tank the previous night.

Then there was the time somebody painted Bill Pearson's white horse coal-black. It was a year before the poor steed got back to her original colour. But I assure you that Bill and I were far too busy to be involved in such nonsense.

Job-wise, Bill had the only paper route in the village, and I was in charge of two cows belonging to the local priest, Father Lambert

Garvin. The first cow, Harmonius, arrived at the Catholic rectory when the good Father traded his 1936 Dodge for a new 1939 Chrysler with a local salesman, Park Dougal. I am not sure how the cow entered the deal, but there was also another item in the transaction. This was a jack which came with the cow. I was to find out what that was for, when I went to milk her for the first time. She had the longest udder I'd ever seen, and her teats were just three inches off the ground. I asked Park how I was ever going to get a pail beneath her, come milking time, and he says, "Just jack her up."

This being the spring of 1939, there was a threat of war hanging over the world and Father Garvin had decided to begin his war effort early by supplying himself with his own milk and butter. As it turned out, it was more of a make-work effort, as it gave me a little spending money and his housekeeper, Anna Quigley, a hell of a lot of extra chores. She had to churn the milk to make the butter and, on the many occasions when they couldn't find me, milk the cow. Now one cow is bad enough, but two cows can become a problem, and it was not long before Harmonius had a daughter, Obediah. So, come summer, both cows were pastured out on the front lawn of the church, and there were many complaints that there was more cow shit tracked through the church than there was on the front lawn.

Getting back to Bill and my social life, we never missed even the most minor affair, whether it be the old movies in the town hall Monday nights, at ten cents a head, or a dance in the Orange Hall on Back Street. The gypsys would arrive every spring and camp at Slys Corners, and the two of us managed to call on them at least once a day. Then, every so often, medicine shows used to come along. They took place up in front of "Si" Steven's Garage. Our favourite was Blackie's Home Remedy Extravaganza, which usually stayed in the village for four days and nights.

Blackie put on quite a show. It would begin with him standing on a platform in front of his trailer, yelling through a megaphone, and saying that no matter what anybody in the audience might be suffering – from lumbago to leaky kidneys – he had a cure. All they had to do was just come to the trailer right after the show and he would prescribe the desired remedy. When enough of a crowd had gathered, he would call on his accomplice, a beautiful, red-haired girl, who would sing a few lonely western songs, accompanying herself on the banjo. After the applause for the singer, Blackie would appear on stage with a big brown bear. He would wrestle with it for about a half an hour, and would always end up the winner. Then he would pull a ten-dollar bill out of his pocket and offer it to any husky farmer who could pin the bear to the floor like he did. I never remember there being any takers. After all this entertainment, the selling of the remedies began.

Now I don't know why, but in those days most people who attended Blackie's show had one complaint in common, and it was Blackie's Pink Pills For Piles that always seemed to grab the public imagination. Perhaps it was the emphasis he placed on the pills when he was giving his spiel. To the best of my knowledge, it went something like this: "If you are troubled by itching rectal softness, do not delay treatment and run the risk of letting this condition become chronic. Any itching, soreness, or painful passage of stool is nature's warning that proper treatment should be secured at once!

"For this purpose, get a package of Pink Pills for Piles and receive instant relief. The pills are taken internally and provide quick relief of itching and soreness. They are not like other remedies, which you rub on externally, and which just irritate the condition. It is the height of folly to think that anyone would risk a painful and chronic pile condition when such a miraculous cure is available at the low price of a buck a jar."

Business was so brisk after the show that Blackie had to engage Bill and me to help hand out the jars and collect the bucks. In exchange for our labour, he always gave us each two full jars. To this day, I can vouch that those pills – if not exactly a cure – were at least a preventative. Never, in my sixty years of rather hard living, did I ever come down with the piles.

Perhaps summer was our busiest time in the district, as there were numerous socials and dances in the town hall at Chaffey's Locks, ball games in every village, and camp meetings at Lake Eloida.

Yet even spring was pretty active. The different schools within a ten-mile radius of Elgin used to call upon Bill's services, as he was quite an accomplished singer. He was always being picked by the local music teacher, Daddy Thrasher, to go around to the different schools and sing at concerts. Bill never liked standing up on the stage alone, so he talked Daddy into letting me stand on the stage with him. Both of them knew that I couldn't sing a lick, so my job was just to move my lips a bit, and go through the motions. It become a duet rather than solo, and we always got great revues from the local critics. I remember Ella Judge, the local correspondent for the *Whig-Standard*, writing that we sang in such unison it was hard to believe there were two of us!

Even the opening of school in the fall was an important day, since you got to see a lot of the farm kids who you hadn't run into all summer. Right from the first day, preparations began for the annual South Crosby School Fair. It was held in Charlie Charland's field, across from where the highschool now stands. Every school in the Township would be represented, each with its own banner. The Elgin school was known as "s.s. No.5," meaning we represented No. 5 school in the Township of South Crosby. I might add that we were all quite proud of our Alma Mater.

Every school in the township used the one and only school yell, known as the "South Crosby War Cry":

> *Horses, cattle, see them grow,*
> *Sheep, swine, Ontario.*
> *Turnips, carrots, corn to pop*
> *Leeds county, right on top.*

The whole purpose of the fair was to give everyone a chance to show off their talents – from growing potatoes to knitting scarves. On the day of the fair, all these goodies were displayed in a big tent, with the contributer's name on them. Three prizes were awarded for each category. You would get a red ribbon for first prize, a green one for second, and a blue one for third. At the end of the judging you would take your ribbon up to the stand where the County Agriculture Representative, Mr. Orsler, would be accompanied by the Chairman of the School Board, George Howard. Then the cash awards for your labour would be dished out: seventy-five cents for the red ribbon; fifty cents for the green one; and a quarter for a blue. All the judging took place after dinner, when the different schools would be marching round and round the field.

One year Bill and I were given the vital task of being banner-bearers. I can't over-emphasize how important a job this was. It was the bearers who led each school and who set the pace. Any chance a school had to ending up in the finals depended on the effort put forth by it's leaders. So much significance was placed on this marching that the first prize was $1.50 – double the other prizes.

Well, the year that Bill and I led the parade, we lost any hope of getting into the finals right at the beginning, when Bob Tate, who was marching directly behind me, stepped on my heels. Down I went, taking the banner and Bill with me. Right off, we knew that we were in bad shape, as we were not at all sure about the quality of our contributions to the tent display.

Like everybody else in the school, we had been given numerous seeds and plants in the spring, compliments of the County of Leeds. But being a little busy at the time, we sold them to our friend, Mac Kelley, who ran the hardware store, at a price he could not have beaten wholesale. So come noon, when everybody was having a big feast beside a campfire, with the teachers and the judges dishing out the food on paper plates, Bill and I sneaked into the tent to do a little rearranging. We had set up our two displays previously: Bill, a flower lover, had begonias, asters, petunias, and sweet peas from Mrs. Pinkerton's garden. I had a vegetable display: carrots, potatoes, onions, and tomatoes from Mert Campbell's garden. As we had gathered our entries in the dark of the night we wanted to see how they stood up against the others. We did a little juggling, and when the prizes were awarded Bill had two firsts for his sweet peas and asters and a third for his begonias. I had a first for my potatoes and two seconds for my tomatoes and onions. So, on a whole, we did not fair too badly, thanks to Mrs. Pinkerton, Mert Campbell, and our little juggling act.

Yet none of these great events were to have such a lasting effect as the time we were invited to go to Kingston and meet the King and Queen. The invitation was not exactly a regal one, but it was the next best thing. Bill's mother, Mae, had a cousin, Eban, who lived in Kingston and worked for the Canadian National Railway. He had quite an important job, icing passenger cars when they came into the Kingston station. (In those days, ice was needed for the refrigerators, and to cool the fans in the cars.) Eban told Bill's mother, well in advance, that if she wanted to bring her son and one of his friends to town the day of the Royal visit, he would see to it that we would have two ringside seats.

Like everybody for miles around, Bill and I started preparing for the big event months ahead of time. I sent to Eatons for a new suit, a three-piecer, vest and all, with short pants. I got Aunt Mary Anne to lend me the money, $5.95, and as soon as it arrived at the post office, I put it on and paraded up to Bill's place. To my surprise he pulls out the suit his mother bought him at Bibbys in Kingston, and it was exactly the same as mine, only it had golf pants. We got to talking, and Bill said with my skinny legs the golf pants would look better on me. As there was a little more cloth in the golf pants than in the short ones, he thought I should pay him a quarter, so I reached into my pocket and a deal was struck.

It became common knowledge around the school that Bill and I would be attending the Royal Visit in a kind of official capacity, having received our invite from a rather important employee of Canada's national railroad. We made it known that we would be posted in front row, centre, seats at the station, and, from this vantage point, we would not only be the first to see the King and Queen arrive, but would also be the last to see them leave.

Every morning, after the Lord's Prayer, the whole school would practice singing *God Save the King*. I don't think my voice improved all that much, but it was one song where I did get to know all the words. We would sing it again just before noon, and twice before we left school at four o'clock.

In every class, the subject of the Royal Visit would come up, whether it was during agriculture or spelling, although the history classes naturally provided the most information. We learned that the Royal Visit to Kingston, once the Capital of Upper Canada, would be the first time that a ruling monarch had visited our land (or His land, as there was some question, even then, who Canada belonged to). Even today, Bill and I are of the opinion that it still belongs to the Indians, but this is just a minority opinion.

Actually it had taken the British Monarchy a thousand years to make it across the Atlantic. Starting with Alfred, who saved the English from being Danes, the long chain then included Canute (a Dane!), who got his feet wet; a bunch of Norman Kings; the Tudors, including Henry VIII, who killed nearly all his wives; Elizabeth I; and then the Stuarts, briefly interrupted by the Cromwell experiment. Afterwards came the House of Orange; the House of Hanover, which produced Victoria, the Empire Builder; and, finally, the House of Windsor. So it was that when George VI and his lovely wife, Queen Elizabeth, stepped down from the train in Kingston, we, the students of Elgin Public School, would be witnessing a first in Canadian history. Believe me, being chosen as a special witness to such an occasion hung heavily upon Bill's and my shoulders for months before the big event.

From Arbour Day, the first Friday in April, onward, the whole population of the village began raking their lawns, slapping a new coat of paint on their houses, scrubbing their verandahs, and daily erecting flags and welcome signs. Now I am not sure why all of this went on, as the closest the King could have got to Elgin, when travelling by rail, was the old Elgin station, a mile outside the village. So I got my Uncle Charlie, the local Secretary of the Liberal Association, to write a letter to Mackenzie King, the Prime Minister of that period. The letter stated that I thought it would be nice if he re-routed the train. I proposed that it should go from Ottawa to Smiths Falls, then up the old C.N. line to Forfar Junction, and afterwards to Elgin station, and then on to Kingston, rather than going by the Canadian Pacific line to Brockville. I never received a response, which made me feel Mr. Mackenzie was a very discourteous person.

Anyhow, the big day finally arrived, Sunday, May 21, 1939. It dawned rather cloudy, but promised to be warm and rather sticky as time progressed. I was up long before daylight, but somehow nothing got moving till much later in the day. At seven o'clock, I was knocking at Bill's door, and for the next five hours we sat on the veranda, all decked out, waiting for his mother. When we weren't practising singing *God Save the King* we were fixing our ties, going over our shoes with a rag, and wetting our hair from a rain-barrel, then combing it different ways, until each of us was satisfied with the other's appearance.

Finally, sharp at noon, Mrs Franklin backed out her '36 Chevy, all polished for the occasion, and Bill and I piled into the back seat. As we started through the village, we noticed a lot of kids along the sidewalks, waiting for buses and rides, so we rolled down our windows and waved at them, just as though we were Royalty ourselves.

True to his word, Eban was at the Outer Station in Kingston to meet us, dressed in his official get-up, stripped overalls, a railway cap, and you could see your face in his black polished boots. Mae left us in Eban's care, telling us she would be back when the Royal Train departed the station. Eban led us about a half-mile down the track, introducing us to other railway fellows as we went along.

Finally, we came to a siding, and he led us over to a box car with the doors open on each side. Both ends of the car were filled with ice. At the doors facing the main line, Eban had put down a couple of bran sacks, and this was to be our ringside seat when the train pulled in. We had a clear view of all trains, whether they came from the east or the west.

So Bill and I climbed up into the car and sat on the bran sacks, with our legs dangling above the tracks, and began our wait. Eban was not sure just what time the Royal train would be arriving, but he told us we were in a good position to watch for it ourselves.

In no time at all there were trains coming from every direction, since as well as thirteen specials from Eastern Ontario, there were also two from Smiths Falls. Besides this, of course, were the regular passenger and freight trains, whizzing by. Well, we didn't take any chances. As soon as we heard a whistle down the line, we jumped off our perch, and headed for the platform, singing *God Save the King* and waving our flags. It was no wonder that, by seven o'clock in the evening, we were both sound asleep on the bran bags when Eban came along and woke us up. He said the train would be arriving in forty-five minutes, as it had just passed through Brockville.

Sure enough, at 7:45 p.m. sharp, the gleaming, streamlined, beautifully finished, blue-and-silver Royal Special pulled into the station. The sun, which had finally decided to make an appearance about 3 p.m., was now going back to bed. But it was still bright enough for those who were at the station to get a clear, daylight view of Their Majesties.

The train had barely come to a smooth stop when the youthful, well-tanned King decended from the observation platform at the end of the car, followed by his beautiful and gracious wife, Queen Elizabeth. Bill and I scrambled up the platform to within a quarter of a mile of their descent and began waving our flags and singing *God Save the King*. I take it that the Royal couple heard us, as they turned and looked in our direction, with both of them waving and smiling. Then it was back to business. The Prime Minister, Mackenzie King, came running up from four cars back, but of course we paid him no heed, as he had not bothered to answer my letter.

Finally, after Mayor Stewart and his wife had presented the Royal couple with orchids, the band of the 14th regiment struck up *Oh Canada* and the King and Queen were led to the royal car, a shiny maroon convertible, with the Royal Standard on its hood. Then off they went to begin their seven-mile journey through the city.

Bill and I returned to the ice car and had just fallen asleep again when Eban returned with two paper plates, heaped with food. He told us that the Royal couple had left word with their chef to send those two young fellows dressed in blue a bit of their supper. It sure was quite a feed. There was smoked salmon, oysters, cooked ham, as well as some little fish-eggs which Bill and I didn't eat, spooning them off to one side. We washed it all down with two big bottles of Elder's gingerale. We then lay down again, and had another little snooze. At nine o'clock Eban was back, to tell us that the Royal couple would be returning in fifteen minutes.

At the station, bright lights had been turned on to illuminate the platform and the Mayor and Mrs. Stewart stood with the Queen for a few minutes on the red, oriental rug which had been placed beside the Royal coach. They were soon joined by the Hon. Norman Rodgers and his wife, the Hon. Tommy Kidd and his wife, along with the Aldermen, their wives, kids, cousins, friends, and close acquaintances.

"Thank you so much," the Queen said to Mayor Stewart's wife, before she followed her husband up the steps to the observation deck of the coach. The Prince of Wales Own Regiment band played *Auld Lang Syne* as the train started to pull slowly out.

There was no sign of Mackenzie King when the train departed. Apparently, he forgot to say thank you, the same way he forgot to answer my letter. But the good Mayor did hear from him later by telegram. "Sorry not to have been able, owing to the sudden departure of Royal train, to say goodbye to Mrs. Stewart and yourself."

The Royal couple, in their majesty, stood holding on to the rail of the observation deck and waved at Bill and me. They were still waving when the coach disappeared around a curve and made its way to Toronto.

Well, after that, trains and cars and buses began leaving the city through the dark of the night, and there was all kinds of confusion. Many people were still stranded in line-ups at two in the morning, but Bill and I were home, cooled out, by midnight. His mother met us just after the train departed, and we shot right out along Division street, took the back road to Westport, and hence to Elgin, hardly seeing another car.

The next day, Monday, May 22, had already been designated as a holiday instead of Victoria Day, May 24. All the students spent it getting ready for Tuesday classes, when everybody who had attended the Kingston ceremony would be asked to give their own account of the historic occasion.

Tuesday morning, Bill and I were the first at school, dressed in our new suits, which were by now a little wrinkled. We waited anxiously for Mr. Charland, the principal, to clank the nine o'clock bell. All the students were assembled in the senior room, but much to our disappointment Bill and I were not called on to give our account till near the very end.

The first on stage were Rose O'H. and Josephine M., who had both watched the ceremonies from the steps of St. Mary's Cathedral. They described how a special platform had been built on the steps for the Archbishop, Michael J. O'Brien, Denis O'Connor, Bishop of Peterborough, and Monseigneur J.F. Nicholson of Belleville, all in their flowing robes. When the King and Queen passed, they both looked up and all the clergy looked down and bowed, then lifted their hands in greeting. The Belleville St. Michael's School Band was the only one in attendance. It struck up with *Annie Laurie* and did it well, according to both Rose and Joey.

Then three older girls, Betty H., Joan O., and Anna D. took to the stage. Like all females of that age, they started in with a lot of flowery language about how lovely the Queen looked, and how the King was a model of masculine dignity in his morning coat, his whole appearance so slim and bronzed and youthful. Then of course, they went on and on about the Queen, how she was always smiling, and looking infinitely lovely in a white silk-crepe ensemble, trimmed with white fox. We had to hear about every detail of her white accessories, a straw hat with veil, trimmed with ostrich tips, with a double string of pearls adding one final touch.

Then Helen Mary O'B., who had just moved from Kingston to Elgin, stood up and told how lucky she had been to have watched the event from Richardson stadium with Elgin students, rather than with her old school, Notre Dame. It seems that the separate school kids in Kingston had been reserved a spot at the stadium, and were supposed to be escorted there at 6 p.m. by the Pipe Band of the Twenty-First Battalion of Kingston, but the band got lost when leading a parade of veterans down to Fort Henry. A mountie finally came to the rescue, and got the kids to their seats, minutes before the Royal couple arrived.

Bill T. and Art M. had been almost as lucky as Bill and I, as they somehow got up the hill at Fort Henry, where they could look down at the whole show. Art told us that this setting, unlike the rest of the city, was quiet, which added to the beauty and grandeur of the occasion. He said it was too dark to get a good view of the King behind the raised glass of the open car, but the Queen, in white, seemed to shine like in a spotlight, and her gloved hand was raised in a friendly greeting, like a warm handshake. Art was always quite a poetic fellow and gave the best account of any of the boys.

Bill, however, noticed other, more practical things. He said the Royal couple were lucky to have got to the Fort at all. It seems that their car didn't make it the first time the driver tried the trick-turn into the grounds. It stalled at the top of the steep hill that sloped down into the St. Lawrence River. Heads began peering out of the cars that were following, as everyone feared trouble, especially when the Royal car began to back up. But it was only a momentary panic. The driver, not used to such large limousines, was just adjusting his steering so he could get through the narrow gate. Everything was fine after that, but the King and Queen seemed more relaxed when they reached the high, isolated hill top. It offered them a little quiet and peace, as well as the chance to get their bearings and to sort of forget any possible tragedy.

Following Art and Bill's account, two senior boys, Bill D., and Ab S. got up. Their story was quite brief. They had decided to be the first of all the Elgin residents to behold the Royal couple, so had caught the old Brockville & Westport bus. They stood on the platform with hundreds of Brockvillians, as well as Mayor C. Gordon MacOdrum. The Mayor was dressed in his finest and had even brought a speech. He was giving it a practice reading when the Royal train whizzed by. Bill and Ab both claimed that the Royal couple managed to race out at the last moment and wave to the people, but there was no mention of that in the next day's papers.

Finally, it was Bill's and my turn to take to the stage, and we began our elaborate account of the visit. Every now and again, Mr. Charland would tell us that we had to get on with it, as it was now well past the dinner hour, but we kept going. We told how the Royal couple had singled us out by waving, before making their tour of the city, and how they had even sent us a Royal dinner. At last, after Mr. Charland had asked us for the fourth or fifth time to cut it short, "Big" Elmer Warren, the school bully, got up from his seat and yelled, "You're both full of .... !" Well, Bill and I went back to our seats, and Mr Charland expelled Elmer for the rest of the week.

So it was, on Sunday, May 21, 1939, William Franklin and Michael J. Murphy became the first residents of the Township of South Crosby to welcome the first British Monarch ever to set foot on Canadian soil.

My kind of people

3

I Begin my Real "Education"

There came a time when I had to leave the little village. Mary Anne was beginning to know some of *my* secrets. Somehow, she knew that I was stealing the odd drink from old Ab's bottle. What was more embarrassing, however, she knew about my secret love life. She felt that I was spending too much time playing hide-and-seek in the old ice-house with a neighbour's beautiful daughter from down the street.

I needed discipline.

To put it plainly, I'd discovered sex. Not that I hadn't known for quite a while that girls were different. Way back, when I was living in Kingston, and my mother was still alive, I noticed, around the age of six, I guess, that girls wore their hair longer than boys and had skirts instead of knickers. Then, when I was seven, I got a new kind of feeling. I just can't explain it, but I seemed drawn like a magnet towards a little blond girl next door. Her name was Jean Murray. I must say when I saw her twenty years later, and she was married by then, I could see I'd had good taste, even at such a tender age.

Everything that mother gave me I shared with Jean – whether it be candy, ice-cream or an apple. When mother bought me a trike, I let Jean ride it all the time and even allowed her to keep it on her verandah. Now mother watched this go on for quite a while and finally one day, she said, "You really like Jean, don't you Micky – do you ever give her a kiss?" "No!" I replied, "Do you think I should?" Mom thought for awhile and then replied, "I think you have given her enough for now."

Well, I started school down the street at St Mary's. My first teacher was Sister Mary Magdalene and I don't ever remember learning any sex from her. Also, it was an all-boy's school.

After the death of my Mom, and I moved to the village of Elgin, things changed quite a bit. I began public school and found that in class boys and girls were mixed about the room together. But, what you noticed most, when you went outside, was this thing about segregation. One side of the school was designated as the girls' side and the other as the boys'. If the teacher caught you on the wrong side, there was hell to pay! This, of course, was long before the Bill of Rights.

Meanwhile, Bill Franklin had slowly become my best friend, and his general knowledge was a bit more advanced than mine. There were times, however, when even Bill didn't have all the answers. One day, when he and I were walking to school, I "seen" a word meaning "intercourse," printed across the Town Hall. Actually, it was another word with the same meaning, but only four letters. I asked Bill if he knew what it meant, and he said he didn't. So then I asked Aunt Mary Anne, and she said to ask our teacher, Miss Kenny. So that's what I did the next day in school. "Well!"said Miss Kenny, who was quite a pert young girl, "I never heard tell of such a word!" But she handed us the old *Webster's Dictionary* that was always on the teacher's desk, and told us to look it up. Finally, after a lot of searching, we told her we couldn't find it. "Then there's no such word!" she replied. "Whoever did that writing was likely a bad speller. It should have read 'luck' and you boys know what that means!"

I think the farm kids got a better education in sex than anyone who lived in the village – their advantage being able to watch the animals mating, birthing, etc. I remember one time Bill and I were sitting on a bench down by the old town pump. Kelly Dier, the butcher up the street, was sitting with us, along with a couple of older residents of the village, who used the bench as a meeting place. Suddenly the conversation was interrupted by a little commotion between two dogs. Father Garvin's little terrier was coupled with a spaniel belonging to a local Orangeman, Bobby McGuire. Well, right off, Bill and I were curious and we asked what they were doing. Kelly, who was never short of an answer, replied, "That's what you call a mixed marriage."

On another occasion, the same thing was happening between Doc Kerr's Labrador and Mart Dunn's old hound, but this time, it was taking place up the street at Uncle Charlie's feed store. I thought perhaps Charlie, who was one of my favourite uncles, would provide a little more information than Kelly did, so I asked him what was going on. Well, at first he seemed a little lost for words. Then, finally, he said, "That old hound of Mart's is getting old and Doc's dog, Duke, is just giving her a little push to help her along."

So Bill and I were gradually picking up bits and pieces of information about sex and the meaning of different words. On Saturdays, we would hang around the feed store and at noon, when the hotel beverage room would open down the street, my uncle Charlie would leave me in charge. I was to answer the phone, take down any orders, tell people what feed was on sale, and then deliver the order to Gerry Dier, who would be out in the grinding mill. Well, this particular day, Charlie and a group of local politicians had been drinking from a bottle they kept in the medicine cabinet, and none of them were feeling any pain. As he was about to leave, he wrote down the prices of the different kinds of feed, along with a foot-note: "On Special Today – Robin Hood by the bag and Aunt Jemima by the box."

Well, the first call I got was from Josephine Jordan, who lived near the Foster's Locks. Josephine was not exactly what you would call a typical farmer's wife. She had come from a rather large city in Western Ontario, was well-educated and quite refined, and never fitted into the life on the farm – always complaining that she never felt all that well. It became a ritual around the village to always ask Josephine how she was feeling before you entered into any conversation with her and, without fail, her answer was either she was "recuperating" or "convalescing."

Anyway, getting back to the phone call – she said that she wanted two bags of shorts, three of ground oats and one bag of middlings – and then asked what was on sale. When I told her that we had Aunt Jemima by the box and Robin Hood by the bag, the phone went dead and although I rang her back three or four times, there was no answer. So, when Charlie came back, I told him what went on and he said, "That's okay, just add a bag of Robin Hood Flour to the order." Of course, I hadn't realized that words like "box" and "bag" could have a different meaning around our district.

I suppose there was never a day a little sex didn't enter the conversation around the feed store, but again, it was often mentioned in such a way that I'm not quite sure I always understood. One of the fellows who used to hang around the office was a retired cheesemaker, named Frank Levine. Frank's memory was going a bit, and although there were not that many cars in the village, everyone that would go by Frank would ask, "Who's that?" Charlie would look up and say "Elswood Bedore." Then someone else would go by and the same thing would happen. After about ten or twelve times, Frank would seem to regain his memory and say, "That Elswood goes by a lot, don't he?"

Besides his forgetfulness, Frank's tolerance for booze was also diminishing, and after he would have a few "shots," he would lay down on the old couch in the office, alongside the stove. One day he was lying there sleeping, with one leg up, when he suddenly opened his eyes and said to Charlie, "Ain't it awful to lose your memory?" Then looking down at his raised leg, he said, "I was dreaming I was having sex with the wife and I forget now whether I was getting on or getting off."

Then there was this problem of a girl being "in trouble." What you noticed was she started putting on a bit of weight, and it was rumoured about she had a tumour. There was one particular year, just before the war, when several girls came up with tumours – a minor plague, one might say. So being a little interested, I asked Doc Feeney, who lived just down the street, if tumours were serious. He assured me they weren't, but told me that all the girls would have to go away for a rest, and then the tumours would disappear on their own.

Well, time went on, and Bill and I were beginning to pride ourselves on our knowledge about sex. Mostly because a few of the girls around the village knew a lot more – girls maturing faster, I guess. Soon the hide-and-seek games we had been playing became a bit of an "orgy." A couple of the girls would let go purposely while we were hiding in the ice-house. This was a sign that they wanted to "pair-off." Now, I'm not going to give you any details, but it was one of the factors that contributed to me being sent away.

As I said before, everyone felt I needed "discipline." So thus I was shipped off to a Jesuit boarding-school in Kingston, the city of my birth. I remember those first few nights crying myself to sleep, thinking of Aunt Mary Anne and my village friends.

My kind of people **4**

My "Education" Continues

The school was called Regiopolis, and was for boys only. For any of you who may be interested, it was also one of the oldest teaching institutions in Canada, dating back to 1832. In that year, Bishop Alexander Macdonnel laid the cornerstone. Being a Scotsman, and well-versed in financial affairs, he then took off to his homeland never to return. For years, the great school of learning was plagued with financial problems, until almost a hundred years later, when it was taken over by the Canadian Jesuits.

It then became a classical institution, where many a scholar was immersed in Greek and Latin, and every graduate was able to say with confidence that Regi meant King in Latin, and Polis meant town in Greek. It is said that the scholars of the time studied Virgil, Ovid, Sallust, and Aesop's fables, as well as reading Livy's Cicero and Horace – but that's all Greek to me, so I won't dwell on it.

Anyhow, after the school was taken over by the Jesuits it became a combination day and boarding highschool, and in 1938 it revived its university charter and launched an Arts course. But to the best of my knowledge only six degrees were ever granted, four in 1941, and two in 1942. Probably the best-known recipient of these rather scarce sheepskins of learning is the well-known columnist with the *Catholic Register*, Father Tom Raby. Perhaps it was because of the war, or for reasons we will never know, but the school diplomas were never deemed important. The important thing was to be able to say in later life that you *attended* this noble institution, whether for one year or five. Scattered throughout the world today are many former students who proudly proclaim, "I was a Regi Boy." Contrary to what you may have heard, the Jesuits were not tough disciplinarians. They taught a boy he must discipline himself or suffer the consequences. Their motto was, "Send me a boy and I will send you back a man." Yet they warned that a man without discipline was a ship without a port, and the sea of life would be just as rough as the man himself wanted to make it. More important, however, was the way they taught a boy how to survive when those battering waves would begin to shatter the outer hull. You learned early that you did not stop and drop anchor, but sailed onward against the elements, till you could find a place to dock and seek help. They warned that it would be a humbling experience, but that was good, for there are only two kinds of people that ever find God – the humble and the simple. People who realize they know nothing, not the clever ones who think they know everything.

Years later, when I myself was floundering in the sea of a wasted life – looking for help, or at least a quiet port to weather out the storm, I got to thinking of all the Jesuits I had known, and which of them had influenced me the most. Then it came to me. It was a lovable old Irish priest we students fondly called "Pop." I had come in contact with many a Jesuit the world deemed more brilliant – including Bernard Lonergan, and his more down-to-earth brother, Greg. Bernard became famous for his towering masterpieces, *Insight* and *The Human Act of Understanding*. That understood, I hope *you* understand my trouble understanding either text. Most of his writings were in Latin, and, like me, he wandered a bit before he got to the point. The point is, I never knew when he had reached his point, so the end was more baffling than the beginning.

Now Pop, he was a different man altogether. He was brilliant in his own right. He taught mathematics and, rather grudgingly, Fifth Form religion. He felt he was wasting his time trying to teach a boy in his late teens what the church wanted him to believe, for it was a time when young fellows were asking themselves what on earth they *did* believe in. "Do not trust the feelings of youth, for they will quickly change – even against your will – but heed the warnings that come from within, or they will haunt you to the end," he would say, over and over again. Although Pop covered the text that was prescribed for the students, he didn't seem to have his heart in it. Instead, he tried to instill in every one of us a hidden, moving power within our own consciences.

Yes, Pop was different. But what was more important to us at the time, he was human. He had a weakness himself, which he carried openly on his breath. He alway smelled of booze. There was many a mother and member of the Women's Auxiliary who was fooled by Pop's breath. He was a tiny elf of a man, who alway wore his beret to cover his bald head, and gold-rimmed glasses to shield his mischievous eyes. He looked like the roly-poly Pillsbury Doughboy, so all the good women attributed the smell of yeast on his breath to the pleasant aroma of fresh-baked bread. He presented no scandal for any who might be easily scandalized. We students knew otherwise. But we also knew that a man who carried his weakness openly would be all-forgiving and understanding. I guess you noticed it most on Sunday mornings, when the students would line up for confession. There would be a never-ending line to Pop's confessional, while the other priests sat yawning and reading their breviaries. His penance was always the same, "Go in peace and do something to help someone less fortunate."

His religion classes would always start out in the same way, too. He would wander into the classroom with his soutane dragging the floor and his head turned towards a window overlooking the parking lot. His class started at eleven-thirty – the last class before noon. Suddenly, out of nowhere, a ragged figure would appear in the lot, and turning to the class Pop would say, "Christ is here." With that he would disappear down to the cafeteria, where one of the good Sisters of St. Martha would always have a lunch packed in wax paper. Then he would head out the basement door to greet his friend.

I remember one day in class as I sat, hidden I thought, behind a big football lineman, Lazardo Garcia. (Laz and three of his brothers were Cubans who attended the school. They now own one of the biggest shipping lines in the world, out of New York.) I had my legs stretched out and my head resting on my desk when Pop began his class, after making his daily delivery. In no time I was sitting bolt upright as Pop began his lecture with the words, "I doubt if there is a fellow in this room that would piss against the wall for Christ. Don't worry He won't need you, but the day will come when you need Him." Then, standing on his tiptoes he peered down at me, and in a softer voice said, "Watch out for slothful habits, as in time you will become unhappy, uneasy, and strained; as deep down you will know there is a richer life. Until you overcome such habits, or at least make an attempt, there will be no peace or haven in which to hide." "Pop," also told us that sex was not a thing that would go away itself but would remain with us quite awhile, till age took care of it, like a lot of other vices. "All of you will think about it, some will use it, others will abuse it, but regardless, it is something that will be with you for a long time. I presume none of you will be growing old here, so I advise that you refrain from any temptation, including the one favoured by Catholic youth, masturbation. While in school you shouldn't find this too hard, as long as you eat your porridge."

Now Pop did not need to elaborate, but for those of you who never attended boarding-school, it was always rumoured that a little saltpeter found its way into the oatmeal. I don't think it improved the flavour, but it did slow a young fellow down a bit.

One student I'm sure that never ate the porridge was a fellow named "Hollywood." I'm not sure where he came from, if I ever knew, but I met him for the first time during my second year. He was playing pool down in the recreation room, taking the boys for their allowances, when a friend of mine, Joe Kelly, came along and said I should check this fellow out. Hollywood was indeed different, he was wearing a zoot suit, wide lapels, billowing trousers, and a loud, flowered tie. Instead of a brush cut, which was popular in those days, he had his dyed blond hair trimmed mohawk style.

Right off, Holly and I became friends, and he let me in on a little secret, he ate glass, whether it be ground-up pop bottles or light bulbs.

It was not long before he became the main attraction around the school, displaying his fondness for glass rather than grass, along with doing a lot of magic tricks.

Then one night it happened. It was a Saturday, late in September and the Kingston fair up the street was winding down. Holly invited Joe and I to go along with him for the closing night and see if we could pick up some girls. I guess since he was on a glass diet, and didn't eat the porridge, he was getting the urge.

We made the rounds until we finally came to the girly show. There was an old barker standing outside this tent with a fog-horn voice, inviting everybody to come forward and buy a ticket to the sexiest show ever staged in North America. "Inside the flaps of this tent," he bellowed, "you will behold one hundred delights!"

Holly walks up to the barker and asks who is in charge of the show. He explains that he is a magician and has a lot to offer. It was between shows, so the barker goes into the tent and comes back with a girl who looked like Lana Turner in a mini, mini, skirt. Right off, Holly begins pulling dollar bills from her ample bosom and, if Kelly and I are surprised, the lady is flabergasted. After handing the nice young thing a fistful of bills, he then takes out a light bulb and starts chewing on it like an apple.

Needless to say, the star of the show was duly impressed, and she gives Holly three passes for the next performance and tells him she will see him right after the final curtain. Taking our turn behind a group of farmers, who kept looking around to see if anyone was watching, and ready to duck out of the line if they were, we finally made our way into the show. It was indeed, quite a performance, and the girls finally got around to showing their all. As they stood there, naked, with the whole audience bug-eyed, a drum suddenly went boom and down came the curtain.

True to her word, "Lana" appeared in front of the tent about ten minutes later, accompanied by two other beauties, Cheryl and Nancy. After the introductions, she invited us into a trailer, parked to one side of the tent. Once we were seated our hostess produced a bottle of rye and six glasses. We sat around a small table to kind of get acquainted. After a bit of small talk, it was no time at all till Lana and Holly were holding hands. Finally they excused themselves, saying they had some important business to do, and they would be back in an hour or so. After they had disappeared behind a partition, I saw Joe moving a bit towards Nancy so I thought I would crowd over a little by Cheryl. I started to look warmly into her eyes but found she was looking coldly into mine. I looked over, and Joe was fairing no better. We all started making little giggling movements and whispering to each other. I decided I was using the wrong approach so I said, "It's a nice night out, ain't it?" "What's nice about it?" they said almost in unison. Cheryl says, "I wish he would come back out, ain't he something?" Well Joe and I finally got the message, so we poured ourselves another drink, while the girls sat quietly waiting for Holly to return.

Finally he shows up, but only for a minute. He tells the girls that Lana wants to see them, and everyone disappears. In about five minutes he returns and says he has some bad news. It seems the girls are not much taken by Joe and me, and he doesn't think it's worth our while to hang around. He then hands us a fistful of dollar bills and says he has some even sadder news. He has decided that boarding-school is not his thing and, as the show is pulling out early the next morning to Syracuse, he thinks it's a good time to start his show biz career. He then goes on to say how much he would miss us, and how sorry he was that he never got around to showing us the trick of eating glass, as he knew that the grub at the school was far from good. Finally, he asks us to pack his clothes when we get back to the dormitory, and leave them on the lawn, in front of the school.

So it was that I received my first rejection from a city girl, and I'm afraid it affected me all my life. I also lost the friendship of the only magician I ever knew, and things around Regi were never the same. I suppose, if that was today, I could have gone to a shrink and told him my troubles, and he would have advised me that all young fellows go through a stage when they are shy with girls. Yet how could I explain that I was not shy with country girls, who were not backward about coming forward.

Every year at Regi there were two big social events, the Regi and Notre Dame formals, held down in the ballroom of the old Lasalle Hotel on Bagot Street. I never remember attending a Regi formal in a social capacity, only as a coat-checker. One time, however, I was invited to the Notre Dame formal by a beautiful girl named Ann, who was boarding at the local convent. I guess she had picked my name out of the football lineup, or seen me play in one of our games at the old Richardson stadium. Due to the helmets and uniforms we wore in those days, everybody looked very much alike, and she decided to take a chance on me.

I did manage to get a lot of information about her, and it was all good. She came from rather a wealthy family in New York, and everyone assured me she would be the belle of the ball. There was only one thing, I was still suffering that inferiority complex regarding big-city girls, and aftermath of my visit to the fair with Holly. As a result I began to worry about a month before the event. I began to visualize rather a long hard night, if she rejected me the way Cheryl had.

About a week before the formal I was sitting down in the recreation room with my friend the "Midget," Charlie M. Now Charlie was a longtime resident of Regi, and he and I used to sneak out now and again and socialize at the beverage room in Portsmouth village. I told Charlie my problem and right away he came up with a solution. He said that I was a far different fellow when I'd had a couple of drinks. Now Charlie was not always the most pleasant of fellows, but who is? (If you ever attended any wrestling matches at Maple Leaf Gardens, you probably have seen Charlie. Paul Rimstead engaged him as an advisor for one of his Irish wrestlers.)

Anyway, Charlie advised me that maybe I should buy a bottle to build up a little false courage. So I told Charlie that I wasn't too flush, since, once I had bought the girl a corsage, I wouldn't have much left. Well, Charlie may have been short of height but he was never short of money, and he said he would look after it for me.

Now listening in on the conversation was a fellow named Jack Major, who now heads the biggest legal firm in Calgary. Jack always had a naturally legal brain, especially when it came to keeping out of trouble, and he said, if I didn't mind, he would like to give me a little advice. Jack had been dating a beautiful French girl who was also at the convent, and he explained that the security down there was pretty tight. It seemed that when you went to pick up your date there was a rather elderly sister, named Sister Rosanna, who sat just inside the door. Although she did not look all that observant, she could smell booze on your breath a mile away, and no girl was allowed out with a fellow who was drinking. "They don't call her "Nosie Rosie" for nothing," he warned.

Well I asked him what he proposed I do, and he said he already had a plan. I should get hold of my friend "Senator Brown," and when I went to pick her up, the Senator could do the honours of going through security and fetching her out to the taxi, where I would be waiting.

Maybe I should fill you in a little on the Senator. He was not an ordinary Regi student, just a fellow who boarded there, and went to business college down the street. It is said that he had tried the Christian Brothers at some place down in Quebec, but had decided to get into the financial end of the church. Thus he was now attending a renowned Kingston business college, while rooming and boarding at Regi. He still wore his Brother's regalia, black suit, shoes and tie. He had that saintly look that every Catholic mother would be proud of, and there was never a hair on his head out of place. He was a daily communicant and never had to go to confession. All the priests used the Senator as an example of what Christianity was all about. All, with one exception, old Pop. One day he and I were sitting outside visiting when the Senator goes by. Right out of the blue he says, "In my day, a fellow used to do what the church told him, or get out. Now we got fellows doing what ever the hell they like, and staying in. This will be some organization when everything is left to a hardened conscience."

I never knew whether Pop knew all the facts about the Senator's private life, such as certain arrangements with me and the boys, but I guess somehow he must have. The Senator you see, had not been to business college any more than a month when he was typing sixty words a minute. The Dean of Studies, Father Crusoe, decided that such talent should not go to waste, so he engaged the Senator to type up all the exams. As the Senator kept acquiring financial knowledge, he decided that he was working rather too cheaply, so he approached me with a plan. He could produce a copy of any exam to be written, if the price was right. As there were many wealthy students in attendance, I informed him that price was no object, as long as I could cut myself and a few of my friends in. So a deal was struck.

As business was thriving, I had no problem approaching the Senator for a little favour. The big night arrived, and everything went according to plan. We grabbed a cab, went to the convent, and taking the corsage, he hustled up to "Nosie Rosie" and presented his credentials – along with his calling card – a beautiful portrait of his favourite saint, "The Good Thief." He then graciously escorted my date to the cab and disappeared.

Well, the first part of the night was not all that smooth. There was little conversation, and you could drive two trucks between us when we danced. Then intermission arrived, we found a table, and I ordered a couple of cokes. I asked her if she would like a little mix.

She replied that she would, so I poured her a good one. In no time, after two or three more mixes, we were talking like long-lost friends and even holding hands. Soon we were dancing cheek-to-cheek, and you couldn't have driven a pin between us. It was an evening I will never forget, and I knew, at last, I had found the love of my life.

We smooched passionately in the back seat of the cab on the way back to the convent. I decided to see her home with a little class, so I escorted her through the front door and into the darkened parlour. I took her in my arms again and began to hold her warmly, when suddenly the lights went on, and there stood Nosie Rosie.

The next night, true to my word, I called the convent, sharp at seven, and asked for Ann. A rather stern voice answered the phone and said, "Ann isn't here any more she was dismissed from the school this morning."

I was heartbroken for years, and although I never did hear from her again personally, my friend Major ran into her several years later in New York. She was happily married with five children. I guess that helps, as I like to think that maybe that night I gave her some ideas.

So the years have passed, and I never did really fall in love again. Just the other night, I was sitting in my apartment, there was a knock at the door, and there stood my neighbour from down the hall with her son Billy. Janet, a divorcee, another Ann if I ever saw one, asked in the way of a greeting if I would mind baby-sitting for a couple of hours. "With you or Billy?" I asked with a smile. "With Billy tonight," she replied, "but maybe some time I will need a little sitting myself." I only needed to look in her eyes to know it was trust not lust.

So there it is, the story of my love life. Although I doubt that you have learned anything, I can assure you that Pop was right when he said that age would take care of a lot of vices. Oh, yes, there is one more quote of Pop's that might interest any of you married couples: "The great thing about marriage is when you fall out of love, it keeps you together till you fall back in again."

I left school some four years later; and I can still hear the words of the old Jesuit rector, Father Crusoe. "Miss Murphy, the Jesuits have a motto. Send me a boy and I will send you back a man. I am afraid with Michael, we are sending back a mixture of many men."

I was lost that first summer I came back to the village. I didn't know what I wanted to do in life. One night I decided to visit one of my childhood idols at his big mansion of a cottage some three miles away. W.K. Bickel, or "Duke," as he was known to his close friends, was President of United Press International, and he summered in the Elgin district for years.

When I reached his cottage he was sitting alone in a rowboat, painting the landscape and drinking from a bottle of scotch.

"Mr. Bickel," I shouted, "Could I talk to you for a minute?"

"Why do you invade my privacy?" he shouted back as he rowed toward me.

When he had docked the boat, I explained to him that I wanted to be a writer – to write about famous men, like him. He did not answer, but glanced toward his mansion and watched as his wife, Mediera, wearing a wide-rimmed old hat, half-stumbled down the cottage steps. By now she was in the twilight of life, but she had been a beautiful woman. He had fallen in love with her and her beauty years ago, when she rode the white horse in the Ringling Circus.

Then finally, looking back at me, he said, "There is no such thing as a great writer or a great artist. They are just ordinary people who reveal the world to others. And there is no such thing as a famous man. Everybody in the world is of equal importance. Some are known better for their accomplishments than others, and become what you call famous. But that's the world's version of success, not mine."

These words linger with me to this day. Then he became even poetic when I asked him why he spent his summers here.

"I come for stillness. Here men cease to think. I contemplate. I love. Love passes knowledge, which answers the deepest need in all of us."

As I left, he shook my hand and said, "If you want to reveal, write about the little things in life. Nobody else seems to get the time. Most of all, write about the people you know best; everyday people, for they are part of all of us."

Over the years, I often thought about Mr. Bickel and his words. During those years, I was to do many foolish things. And it was only after I'd changed a lot of my bad habits that I was ready to begin this book. But maybe, if I hadn't had a few of those habits in the first place – there wouldn't have been a book to write!

My kind of people

Bill Cook

Before I get into telling you what happened to me after I left the Jesuit College, I think you should hear the story of my all-time hero – Bill Cook.

Every child needs a hero – somebody he looks up to, someone he imitates, and worships. Mine was William Osser Cook, member of the Hockey Hall of Fame, who became such a part of me that his image is still firmly implanted in my mind. Bill starred, along with his younger brother Bun, with the New York Rangers from the time the old "Broadway Blue Shirts" were assembled in 1926 by Conn Smythe, till he retired as a player in 1937. Centered by the great Frank Boucher, they formed one of the most potent lines of hockey that ever existed.

Around Kingston during the Thirties Bill was everybody's hero, and his picture, along with other hockey players of the day, came wrapped in penny bubble gum. It was Bill's picture that every kid coveted and it became top currency, a piece of barter among the children. So much so that a picture of Bill was good for dozens of other portraits of players of that era.

I had three. One that I always carried in my little black, worn wallet. One that I locked in my toy safe with my other treasures, and the other one which I gave to my mother, just in case. I know now that Bill was mother's hero, too, for she would clip everything she could find written about him and read them to me. Then she would put the clippings away with the picture and say, "I nursed Bill's mother one winter, when she became sick in New York."

We kids in Kingston, like every kid across Canada, played shinny on the street with frozen road-apples, as horses were plentiful in those days. On our street, Brock, we used to play our games in front of the fire hall which still stands. Somehow, my dear friend the Fire Chief, Mr. Armstrong, knew about my great infatuation for Bill and he got me a Ranger sweater, adorned with his famous "Number Seven." I wore that sweater for years, and when I finally grew enough to partly fill it, it had been patched and darned so often that there was nothing left. After moving some thirty miles away to the village of Elgin, my Aunt Mary Anne, who became my second mother, knitted me another.

In Elgin, I was able to obtain three more pictures of Bill, as the village hero was a Chicago Black Hawk player, Vic Ripley, who had been born there. I suppose today that Vic would be classed as a journeyman hockey player, but to the children of the village he, too, was a star. Vic was to score the overtime goal when Chicago defeated the Maple Leafs in the first game ever played in Maple Leaf Gardens, and later was a very successful coach in the United States college hockey. I had collected several of his pictures, so I had no trouble trading, even up, for one of Bill.

When I wasn't playing shinny, I would stand in the kitchen facing a mirror with my hockey stick and all, and practice the intimidating scowl that hung on Bill's face in all those pictures. I was lucky I got to see my hero several times as a kid, and also after I went to boarding school, because one of his sons, Chuck, was there too. I never saw him play, but I never missed a radio broadcast when the Rangers were on. I am glad now that there was no television. Listening to the radio on those cold winter nights, I formed my own image of the way Bill dominated the play when he stepped on the ice. Images that, I suppose, only a child and his imagination could create in living colour. Images that still remain with me today.

So there I was, in 1985, sitting alone, reminiscing about my childhood, when I began to recall Bill, and the pleasure he had given me all those years. For some reason, as a man, I had never been able to walk up to him and tell him how much he meant to me. I would always stand back in awe and say to myself, "Maybe the next time." But somehow I knew that day was *the* day, for there might not be a next time. So I picked up the phone and called Bill at his Kingston address. The voice was still strong but a little distant at first, until I told him who I was and how he had been my hero for all of those years. "Come down for a visit after Christmas," he said. 'But don't bring anything stronger than brandy. I'm eighty-eight you know, and I am slowing down a bit."

Two days after Christmas, accompanied by Joe Fahey, whose Uncle Jimmie had played with Bill in the Soo, I called on him. As we walked down the hallway, we saw him standing waiting, scowl and all, still a powerful man with arms and legs like cord-wood and fingers like oversize cigars. Slowly the scowl faded when I took his hand, and changed to a humble smile when I clung to it and said, "Bill, you're still my hero." "That's nice to hear," he replied, as he led the two of us into his apartment. As I followed I thought how nice it would be if the world could see that smile. Too often, Bill had been portrayed as a leatherneck, a tough, aggressive warrior who gave no quarter and asked none in return. Only his family, close friends, and children knew the real Bill Cook. The man who had known fame, but – what was more important – had been able to handle it. The man who, through it all, wanted to be known as just a simple guy at heart. My kind of person – the kind Mr. Bickell had once told me to write about.

As Bill talked, taking me through his childhood, I was to realize this even more. His early years in Kingston were spent on Rideau Street, near the old tannery. A tough district, where poor Irish and Scotch settlers lived and laboured. As a child, Bill soon learned to take care of himself, for to stroll up the street in that district was like taking your life in your hands. Daily there would be fights, and they would go on all day, for two days, and sometimes even a week. Only the fittest survived.

The summers would be spent skinny-dipping in the muddy marsh, known as Keatings Pond, where the Rideau and St. Lawrence River meet. Here, the kids would swim the murky water, amid the wild fowl and muskrats, parting the cattails and dense weeds. In winter, the same marsh became a skating rink. So it was here that Bill experienced the freedom and elation that came with donning his first pair of skates and gliding over the ice. The skates had belonged to his sister, Dora, and even with four pairs of old wool socks, they were far too big. But, oh, what they meant to a child! Gradually, Bill's natural ability grew, and in his own words, "It gave me an exhilarating feeling, as if I was to take off like a wild goose in flight."

In November, once winter set in, those skates would remain tied to Bill's feet every waking hour when he was not at school, even as he ate his meals, till the spring came, and the warm March sun changed the skating surface back to a muddy pond.

Bill had his heroes, too, among the local hockey players and he used to sneak into the old Jock Harty Rink to watch them play. Guys like the Millans, Richardsons, Al Davidson, and Buddy Hunt. And after a few winters of skating on his pond he got that deep, knowing feeling, something most children long for; the realization that some day he would be good enough to play with the best. And so it was. By his early teens he was already playing with the top amateur teams around Kingston alongside his heroes.

Fate was to postpone Bill's ambition, when the First World War broke out and he went overseas with the Canadian Artillery with Conn Smythe, and a later teammate with the New York Rangers, "Ching Johnson." Bill saw action at Ypres, Vimy Ridge, The Somme, and Flanders. He then joined a group of Canadians attached to the White Russian army and fought the Bolsheviks near the Arctic Circle in 1919.

After the war, Bill did not know what he wanted to do in civilian life. He had received his primary-school education at St. John's, and his highschool had been Regiopolis College in Kingston, then located on King Street, where the new Empire Life building now stands. After that, he had gone to the University of Ottawa, where he starred on the hockey team, and then to Kemptville Agricultural School.

Finally he remembered an old army buddy telling him about the opportunities that the wild, unsettled West offered a young fellow seeking a challenge. So it was off to Saskatchewan with his Veterans

Allowance to the City of Regina. then north, 160 miles, to the desolate hamlet of Lac Vert. After that, he trudged another thirty miles to his idea of heaven, 460 acres of virgin land, surrounded with lakes, streams, and forest. Fish and game of every species were plentiful. Yes, there were even muskrats, – his old swimming companions in that original Rideau swamp near Kingston. "It was so desolate and isolated that I doubt like hell if even the native Indians had ever set foot in that particular territory," he told us during our visit.

But the winters brought everything to a standstill: not even brass monkeys ventured out. Sitting around in his wilderness cabin with time on his hands, Bill began to re-live the past and to dream of what shape the future would take. Once again he was haunted by that childhood revelation: "I'm good enough to play with the best." So, one day, he packed his suitcase and headed east to Ontario, then north to Sault Ste. Marie, where he joined the old Soo Grey Hounds, and began his illustrious hockey career.

It was here that he met the love of his life, a pretty colleen with eyes that twinkled like those northern stars. It was love at first sight, a love that lasted for decades. The two celebrated their sixtieth wedding anniversary in 1982. Claire had passed away two years before I visited Bill and, as he talked about her, his voice choked a bit and memory of her moistened his ageing eyes. Eyes that have witnessed both pain and glory.

There would be four children from that marriage. Jim, the oldest, whom I never met, but whose picture is a spitting image of his father. Billie Marie, the only girl, died in 1970, taking part of her father with her. Then there was Chuck, the one I knew the best, having attended boarding school with him. And finally, the youngest brother, Murray. As Bill, Joe, and I sat visiting, Bill's love for those children unfolded: "Every man should marry and have children and know what it is to love and be loved by a family. There's nothing, absolutely nothing, that I need now in life that my kids and their families don't give to me."

In the Soo, Bill starred in perhaps the greatest amateur team ever assembled. All the players, with the exception of my friend, Joe Fahey's Uncle Jimmy, who lost an eye when hit by an opposing player's stick, were later to turn pro. It was not long before Bill Cook was making headlines in amateur hockey, and soon nearly every professional team was trying to sign him.

The first to approach the great right-winger were the Calgary Tigers of the old Western League. A wire story, originating in the West, proclaimed that after the 1921-1922 season, Cook had shunned all offers to turn pro, and returned to his farm in Lac Vert. But Lloyd Turner, manager of the Calgary Tigers, knew the Cook boy of old, and his remembered abilities as a puck-chaser and scorer. So he dispatched his romantic, hustling coach, "Rosie" Helmer, who wasn't averse to downing a few on occasion, north to Lac Vert.

Rosie arrived at Lac Vert late one night in the fall of '22. It was colder than a chunk of ice on a burning cheek, and snowing like the Lord was already tired of his creation and planning to bury it beneath a few tons of white fleece. Rosie stopped at Lac Vert just long enough to pick up a little "antifreeze" and then hired a livery to drive him out to the Cook ranch. He arrived about three in the morning, and finally managed to get Bill's brother, Bunny, who was also staying there, out of bed. Bunny aroused Bill and the session began.

A few days later Rosie returned to Calgary a little worse for wear. When he got off the train, the first guy he ran into was his boss, Turner. "Well, did you have any luck?," Lloyd greeted his henchman. "Sure did," replied Rosie. "Well did you get Cook to sign a contract?" "Not exactly," replied Rosie. "I think I lost my pen on the way up, and I'll be damned if I could find a pencil or even a piece of paper around that joint of theirs."

What Turner told Helmer that night was never made public. But when it was later announced that Bill Cook had signed to play with the Saskatoon Sheiks, you need little imagination to visualize the conversation that must have gone on between Turner and Rosie.

After Bill's four-year sojourn with the Western League, the East beckoned. That final year in the West saw the Sheiks lose to the Victoria Cougars, who went on to win the Stanley Cup. Tex Richard, the old promoter, began forming a team to play in Madison Square Gardens in New York, and he hired Conn Smythe to assemble his squad. Bill had been contacted by the Montreal Maroons, and he was heading East to talk to that club when he was intercepted at Winnipeg by Connie Smythe. The meeting resulted in Bill and Bunny signing with the Rangers, receiving bonuses of $5,000 and $3,000, respectively.

Bill told Smythe that since he'd now got the two Cooks, he had better also get ahold of a fellow named Frank Boucher, if he was looking for someone to centre the line. Bill had played against Boucher, a star centre with the Vancouver team, who was about to sign with Boston. When he met with Boucher in Ottawa, Smythe was disappointed to say the least. Boucher looked so small and thin that he doubted if the little fellow could carry two hockey sticks at the same time. For once however, the stubborn Smythe was to accept someone else's advice, and thus one of the greatest lines of hockey history was assembled.

Gradually Smythe kept adding players. First he sought out a goalie, and then he came up with big Lorne Chabot from Port Arthur. Lorne was later to join that great Ranger squad, but he did not start in the first game. That distinction fell to a fellow by the name of Winkler.

Bill laughed as he talked about Chabot. The big fellow was exceptional in every way but one: he couldn't skate. When he came out on the ice he would cling to the boards, and then proceed, hand-over-hand, hanging on for dear life till he reached the end of the rink. When he would get directly across from the "twine" (the net, for the uninitiated), he would make a mad dash for crease, hoping to grab onto the goalposts before he fell down. Sometimes he would not make it all the way, and would end up crawling to his position. But once in place, with his skates dug in, and with one of the posts for support, he became one of the greatest goal-tenders of all time, surpassed only by the immortal George Hainsworth, in Bill's opinion.

Then came the defense, Ching Johnston and Taffy Able. Ching was a rough-tough body-checker, a two-way man who could carry the puck and who was not averse to using a little muscle when the occasion called for it. Off the ice, he was a gentleman through and through, and had a wife who looked like a movie actress. Taffy was the only American on the squad, having been born in Sault Ste. Marie, Michigan. He was also a college graduate, and not only performed admirably on the ice but handled a lot of the new club's business transactions.

Over the years, the subs (or alternative players) were to change quite often. But one that still stood out in Bill's memory was Butch Keeling, not only for his hockey ability but for his perseverance. Bill roared with laughter, as he told about one night in Boston when Butch displayed his greatest show of courage and determination.

It had been a rough, hard-fought game with unusually brutal body-checking throughout. Ching was knocking down bodies at one end of the rink while Lionel Hitchman, the great Boston defenseman, was laying them low at the other.

Butch was known for his great puck-control, and once he retrieved the disk, it seemed to stick to him like a fly to a donkey's ass. Ragging the puck, he would head across the Chicago blue line only to be met by Hitchman, who would promptly send him flying. Somehow, during his flight into orbit, he was always able to land on the puck, so he would get up again and proceed to make another attempt in the same direction. Hitchman would be waiting, and again Butch would be launched skyward. After four or five launchings he was getting a little played out. Finally, the whole Ranger bench were on their feet with Bun Cook yelling the loudest, "Butch, for Christ's sake, try changing your course, make a circle, and go in the other side." Butch, however, ignored their pleas, and once more would take off into outer space. This time his flight was even higher. When he landed he was a little short of oxygen – and had to crawl to the Ranger bench, where the boys stood waiting to retrieve his racked body.

Yes, there were plenty of laughs on that early Ranger team. Although it was during Prohibition, there was no shortage of booze if you were a movie star, an athlete, or a celebrity. There was a famous hotel on 48th Street, where the élite of the time bedded down. However it was not the elegant rooms of the establishment that the Ranger team patronized but the basement, known as the Yellow Door. Here the celebrities of the day passed away many a happy hour. As Damon Runyon once wrote: "There was never a team like those early Rangers, they could .... all day and skate all night."

But New York was never a place for an Orangeman and teetotaller like Smythe, with the Irish Micks just about running the town. Richard and his partner, Colonel Hammond, were soon wise to Smythe, yet never once did they divulge their reservations about the man. But one day, after Conn had done the leg-work, a fellow with the same name as the patron saint of New Yorkers quietly appeared on the scene.

Contrary to what a few Toronto writers of the time believed, Lester Patrick, the "Old Silver fox," was not Richard's yes-man. He was a scholarly, quiet gentleman who had played with the best and who knew the game better than anyone then or since. He was a man with few faults of his own, who could shut one eye and sometimes two when it came to judging others.

As for Bill, he always kept a warm spot for Con Smythe. He found him an honest, knowledgeable hockey man and never came to Toronto without paying him a visit. Yet, as a hockey expert, he agreed no one even came close to the old "Silver Fox."

What a time that was to be living in New York – especially if you were a sports fan! Tunney had just become heavyweight champion of the world, having defeated Jack Dempsey. Ruth and Gerig were the stars for the Yankees, and Earl Sandy was the world's top jockey. Red Grange, "The Galloping Ghost," was amazing everyone with his football exploits. If you were a fan of the arts, *Abie's Irish Rose* was playing in the theatres, and you could see Victor McLaughlin playing in *Mother Machree* on 44th Street.

So it came about that the first game in Madison Square Gardens was played on November 15, 1926, and all the celebrities of the day were in attendance. It was to be the New York Rangers against the Montreal Maroons, and it was billed as a charity game to aid Grosvenor House, a new establishment for the poor. If there was to be any charity, however, it was not displayed on the ice, as the game set a record for the number of penalties handed out. They amounted to eighteen, breaking the old record established the year before on St. Patrick's Day, when the same Maroons and the New York Americans staged a fist-fight, better known as a donnybrook. Lou Marsh was the referee, and for some reason he used a cow-bell rather than a whistle to call the play. Why? I suppose some of you might ask. Well, nobody seems to remember. I do recall Mike Rodden, another referee of that era (later sports editor of the Kingston *Whig-Standard*) say that it was then a prerequisite to consume enough alcohol to keep saliva from freezing in the whistle. So I take it that Lou had not yet been introduced to the Yellow Door, or was playing it safe, as there were no breathalizer tests in those days, to tell a fellow when he was blowing a thousand.

That game was to prove quite a shock to the New Yorkers. Somehow, the local sports writers had neglected to do their homework, and all were prophesying a walk-over.

WORLD'S BEST MEETS WORLD'S WORST AS RANGERS MAKE THEIR DEBUT IN THE GARDENS" screamed the headlines in the sports pages. But it quickly became apparent that the new Ranger squad was far more powerful than anyone had dreamed. The big right-winger, Bill Cook, who had had that dream as a child, was not long in proving it. He was to score the only goal in the game, and next day he was the talk of Broadway. The big winner was not only good enough to play with the best – he *was* the best!

The game had everything, from the moment when Miss Lois Moran, a movie star of that era, presented Captain Bill Cook with a hockey stick, just prior to the opening face-off. Each team had its own band, and as was the custom, the Ranger group struck up with *The Star Spangled Banner* as the Rangers themselves, attired in their new uniforms of blue and red with white stripes, skated out onto the ice. They were followed by the Maroons, who naturally received most of the applause. The predominantly Irish-American crowd loved those fighting, pugnacious Maroons, whose actions are best portrayed in the words of the old poem:

> *Irishmen are crazy.*
> *All their wars are merry,*
> *And all their songs are sad.*

But that night, the Rangers quickly established themselves as the kind of team the New Yorkers could take to their hearts. Frank Boucher, the smallest man in the club, discarded his gloves early in the game, and went at Big Bill Phillips of the Maroons in a wild battle. Franky got the best of the fisticuffs till Phillips hit him across the neck with his stick, costing him a gash worth eight stitches. Both were sent off for five minutes and later fined, Boucher heading for the dressing room for repairs, and Phillips to the penalty box. Then it was Ching Johnson and Nels ("Old Poison") Stewart squaring off, and on and on it went until finally the first period came to an end.

During the intermission, a colourful ice ballet was personally conducted by Miss Katy Schmidt, for the benefit of anyone in the crowd who might be interested in the finer things in life. But most of the fans waited impatiently for the beginning of the second period, to see if these Rangers were for real.

They weren't long in finding out. Ching Johnston skated out with a patch over his left eye, covering the five stitches inflicted by "Old Poison's" stick. Undaunted, Johnston took up his aggressive play, laying the opposition low at the Ranger end of the ice, and narrowly missing scoring at the other on two occasions, when he barged through the Maroon defense.

Maybe it is time that I let Seabury Lawrence of the *New York Times* describe some of the action in that second period:

> Bunny and Bill Cook playing Wings, with Frank Boucher at centre, distinguished themselves throughout the period by their dazzling skating and clever stick handling. Bunny, a slim, youthful player, displayed some of the most brilliant hockey of the evening, and seems to be the making of a star in the future. It fell to his older brother Bill, however, to score the only goal of the game, with less than two minutes to go in the second period when the big Winger drilled one home from a beautiful pass by his brother Bun.

The house caved in. The test was not over however. Could the "Blue Shirts" hang on? As the team skated out on the ice for the final period, the roar of the crowd was deafening. Again it became a bashing, knock 'em down affair, with each player getting a piece of the other. Even Referee Marsh would end up on the ice, to the delight of the crowd, when he was bowled over by "Burly" Rocco, a Ranger substitute.

Time and time again, Goalie Winkler stopped everything thrown his way by the Maroons, led by Stewart. Taffy Abel and Ching Johnston almost became goal-tenders themselves, blocking numerous shots, then clearing the puck to Bill, Bun, and Franky, who by now were content to dump the puck into the Maroon zone – with the exception of one last surge. Ching grabbed the puck and, breaking cleanly, headed for the Maroon end of the ice with Frank Boucher in hot pursuit. Inside the blue line, Ching passed the puck back to Boucher and then crashed into Goalie "Praying Clint" Benedict, with the latter falling heavily onto the ice. Frankie lifted the puck into the empty net, but the goal was not allowed.

The cow-bell sounded and the game was over. The Rangers had performed a miracle, defeating the heavily-favoured Maroons 1-0. New Yorkers had a new sports team to worship – "The Broadway Blue Shirts" were on their way. And a new star was born – William Osser Cook.

Following that first game the Rangers quickly established themselves as a team all New Yorkers could be justly proud of. What was more important, they became symbolic of everything heroes are made of, the underdogs who overcame tremendous odds, and went on to fight and conquer. All that season, they were contenders in a strong six-team division.

The next year, they were to do the impossible – they won the Stanley Cup.

Oh, what a series! The playoffs between those same two teams went the limit of five games. There was everything: spectacular plays, fights, and great goal-tending by Chabot, who by now had joined the Rangers, and by Clint Benedict of the Montreal Maroons. Perhaps the incident that was talked about most, and still receives wide publicity, involved Patrick. The Maroons had won the first game 2-0, and in the second period of the second game, with neither team having scored, Nels, "Old Poison" Stewart broke in alone on Chabot and fired a bullet that caught the big Ranger goalie in the left eye. Chabot went down, and right away the Rangers were in trouble as he was carried off the ice and taken to hospital.

The game was delayed for several minutes as the two teams headed to their respective dressing rooms. The Rangers were in a real dilemma. There were no substitute goalies at that time, and a team was not allowed to bring in an outside goalie. After several minutes delay, who skates out, decked in goal-tender's regalia, but Lester Patrick? The crowd of some fourteen-thousand fans was stunned. And Lester who had never played goal in his long hockey career, managed to stop the first two shots, which had looked like sure goals. Well, right away, even the Maroon fans changed their allegiance, and were cheering the forty-five-year-old Lester, who had more than risen to the occasion, Time and time again, the Old Fox dwarfed the opposition, stopping everything thrown his way.

Finally the period ended and the third period began. Midway in the stanza, Bill took a pass from Frankie Boucher and drove it home. Was a miracle about to happen? Could the Rangers hang on? A hush came over the crowd as the two teams fought on.

With six minutes to go, "Old Poison" broke in on Lester all alone and tied the game! At the end of regulation time, the game remained tied; and as they went into overtime it was announced that the team that made the first score would be the winner. After minutes of overtime play, Ching Johnston stole the puck after a Maroon onslaught, and passed it to Frankie Boucher. Frankie skating in alone, decked Benedict and fired it home. There was bedlam in the forum as the Ranger players surrounded Patrick and carried him off the ice. Who could believe rabid Montreal fans cheering a New York victory?

In the next game, the Maroons were to come back and defeat the Rangers 2-0, but the following game saw the Rangers tie the series at two games each, when they defeated the Maroons 1-0. Finally, the last game was slated for April 14. The headlines in the sports pages at the time read, "BILL COOK HAS A SEVERE CHARLIE HORSE." The story then went on to say that Cook was in real trouble, with a badly bruised leg that was causing him severe pain. Every effort was being made to have the muscle massaged into place, and the pain baked out, so that Cook could make one more of his many gallant efforts.

Reminiscing about this crisis in his career, Bill forgot whether or not they used a hot iron, or oil-of-wintergreen externally, or old Rosie's antifreeze internally, to do the job. But in any event he was able to dress and to star in the deciding game. And what a game it turned out to be!

It was Standing Room Only that night, with tickets going for a fortune in Depression money – as much as $35 a seat – the biggest moment in hockey history up until then. A throng of 14,000 witnessed the game, amid scenes of wild excitement, thrills, and dramatic play, as the New Yorkers defeated the Maroons in a savage and bitter battle – 2-1.

It was Frank Boucher who scored both the Ranger goals, on passes from Bill. Joe Miller, the Ranger substitute goalie, stopped dozens of Maroon rallies as they swarmed around the Ranger net. Time and time again Bill, Bun, and Boucher were to break the Maroon defense, only to be stymied by Clint Benedict.

With only a few minutes to go, there was a wild rally at the Ranger net and Miller, scrambling in every direction, lost his stick. Johnson and Able, playing so aggressively that they were knocking bodies in every direction to prevent a Maroon goal, were both sent off for penalties. It looked like it was all over. Then Frank Boucher stole the puck and, in a solo rush, put the Rangers ahead 2-0. Another calamity followed. Bill was sent to the penalty box for crosschecking Nels Stewart. With the Rangers short-handed, "Old Poison" Stewart immediately passed to Phillips for the Maroons' only score. The Rangers were still down to five men, but the Maroons could not crash the last stand taken by the heroic Blue Shirts as the game drew to a close. And so it was that they were presented with Lord Stanley's Cup for the first time.

After it was all over a *New York Times* correspondent was to make some remarkable comments. He described the upset as a game won by sheer courage – a gallant test of guts, speed and, above all, brains. How often have you ever heard the words "brains" being used to describe a hockey club, then or now? Yet that is exactly the way that not one, but two New York writers portrayed the team. Going further, they went on to say that, it was grey matter and speed against blinding aggressiveness and ferocity – and grey matter won.

Prior to the creation of this great Ranger team, athletes as a whole were thought of as individuals who depended on physical prowess, with brawn defeating brains. Patrick realized early that he had a strong, speedy, physical team. But what was more important, most of his players were endowed with something far more vital to success: comprehension and quick response in any situation.

When Bill was interviewed, he kept using the word anticipation, to describe the alert but relaxed response necessary to make a quick judgement – the ability to understand a certain situation before reacting. Bunny and Frankie Boucher had it, so did Ching and Taffy – and the big goalie Chabot, who couldn't even skate. There is little doubt that Bill himself was endowed with the same gift and, over the years, he developed it even more. In describing all the great players of the day – Eddie Shore, Howie Morenz, Nels Stewart, Hainsworth, and Newsy Lalonde – Bill was to use the word anticipation as the key to their great success.

Yet pure guts were also an important factor in that great Ranger victory. If ever an underdog team was in bad shape, it had to be that particular squad: Bill with his charley horse; Ching Johnson with a leg, nose, and eye injury; and Bun Cook, suffering a severe cut in the right foot. It was not long before the goalie Joe Miller, who replaced the injured Chabot, was also injured, only a couple of minutes into the game, when he was struck in the right eye, and felled by a shot from Hooley Smith of the Maroons. Chabot, who had managed to get a temporary release from the Royal Victoria Hospital, sat in the stands to cheer on his teammates, returning to the hospital immediately after the game.

Five years later, the same team, with a change in goalie and substitutes, were to capture their *second* Stanley Cup in Toronto on April 13, 1933. This time the headlines read: "CROWD OF 14,000 SEES RANGERS DEFEAT TORONTO MAPLE LEAFS 1-0 IN TORRID STRUGGLE THAT WENT 7 MINUTES AND 34 SECONDS INTO OVERTIME."

From the outset, the Leafs attempted to dominate the play with their great line: Jackson, Primeau, and Conacher. But time and time again they were stopped in their tracks by the defensive play of Ching Johnston, Earl Seibert, and little goalie Andy Aikenhead. Andy had replaced Chabot as the Ranger goalie, and big Lorne was now guarding the nets for the Maple Leafs. Finally the Leafs, unable to penetrate the defense, or beat the brilliant Aikenhead, began rifling long shots at the Ranger goalie, hoping to catch him off-guard. But Andy turned back everything thrown his way, whether by a longshot or close in. In all, he stopped a total of forty-eight shots, compared to Chabot at the Toronto end with thirty-four.

Three periods were scoreless, with Alex Levinsky and King Clancy rising to spectacular heights for the Leafs, and Ching and Earl Seibert covering the Leaf rushes with their crushing style. Finally regulation time ended in a scoreless tie. Sitting in the Ranger dressing room, Lester Patrick outlined his strategy. He cautioned his players not to gamble, but to wait for a break and make the Leafs come to them, and so the overtime began. At five minutes into overtime, Alex Levinsky and Joe Thoms were both sent to the penalty box, and "The Silver Fox" finally got the break he had been waiting for all night. He put five forwards on the ice, and the quintet began battering away at the Leaf net. Levinsky's exile was almost up, and he was just beginning to return to the ice, when Butch Keeling garnered the puck. On this particular play, not even his old enemy, Lionel Hitchman, could have stopped him, as he broke through Red Horner and King Clancy and skated in on the Leaf net. Horner swung back after Butch, in a final attempt to grab the puck, but skating up from nowhere was Bill. Not breaking his stride, the Ranger Captain took Keeling's pass and, as the big Chabot tried to come out of the cage and topple Bill, the big right-winger lifted the puck swiftly into the far corner of the net.

As the Rangers stood at their bench, waiting to mob Keeling and Bill, nobody was shouting this time, "Butch, you should have gone in the other side," as the perseverance he had displayed all of those years had at last paid off. The crowd was silent for several minutes, but then it suddenly broke into a standing ovation, in appreciation of Keeling and Cook. So it was at thirty-seven, when most hockey players are long retired, Bill Cook became the best right-winger of the day and, in the opinion of many, of all time.

Bill continued to star for the Rangers for another four years. During that time, the league became even rougher and more aggressive, if that were possible. It was then that Bill gained his reputation for being leatherneck, a toughie, a fellow to stay clear of in the corners. His aggressive image followed him everywhere he went. He laughed as I read out a piece written about him by a New York writer: "Bill Cook is the best street-fighter of his time – a man who can take you out with one punch. All that is required is for his opponent to name the weapon – be it a brick, a club, or his fists. If I were to be in a barroom brawl there would not be a man around whom I would rather have behind me."

Bill smiled, "I don't exactly believe that" he said, "but I was no daisy. I guess I learned early in life, playing behind that outhouse at St. John's school, that a fellow had to stand up and be counted. Yet most of the time, it was just intimidation. You would skate up behind a fellow who might be giving you a little trouble, and tell him early in the game what would happen if he didn't change his ways, but after the game it would be forgotten. There were guys like Shore, however, with whom you had to take a more aggressive approach. Eddie did not tolerate very much, even when it came to conversation. I did not talk to him often, on or off the ice, but I guess we both knew our place. Don't get me wrong however, Shore was class when he came down from the West, and I doubt if there ever was a better defenseman."

When I referred to other stories I had heard about his aggressiveness, Bill quietly refrained from answering my questions. Two stories that were reported nationally were the wild brawl, staged with Nels Crutchfield, during the Stanley Cup playoffs with the Maroons in 1935. Crutchfield received eight stitches and was knocked unconscious. The other story concerned a time when Bill was coaching in Cleveland, and one of his players was unfairly felled by an opponent. When the other players failed to come to the guy's rescue,

Bill donned a uniform in the second period and roughed the ruffian up enough to put him in the hospital.

But once the battles were fought, they were forgotten, and that's the way he wanted it, then and now. "You fought with a fellow one night and drank with him the next." So it is perhaps enough to say that Bill could take care of himself (or his pals), when taking care of yourself meant survival. Today the word is against doing any physical damage to a star. But in those days it was just the opposite. The opposition went after the strongest link in a team's chain, hoping to weaken the team and gain an edge.

Following that second Stanley Cup victory, Bill was to star four more years. Then, at the age of forty-one, his legs succumbed to years of being strained to their utmost, and he retired with his brother, Bun, who was eleven years his junior. Bun, too, had developed leg and hip problems which was why his career ended with Bill's. Then it was on to coaching and managing in Cleveland, good years that Bill truly enjoyed. Finally, the call came from his friend, Frankie Boucher, who Bill had been instrumental in bringing to the Rangers. Frankie was now manager of the Rangers, and the old six-team league had now become twelve. Good hockey players were scarce, and the days of heady hockey, stick-handling, passing, and heavy body-checking were almost over. Things didn't really work out, and Bill was to be coach for less than two years. When he left, there were the usual stories that he, and his lifetime friend, Frankie, could not get along, and that Bill left with great animosity towards Boucher. But as Bill was to tell me while we talked, never once had he ever perceived Frankie as anybody but his closest friend. "We lived together, played together, drank together and yes, even .... together."

Perhaps, at the time, if Bill did feel a little bitter, he accepted it quickly as just something else that happens in life. Again he smiled a bit, as he told me how it took just one sentence to dissolve the partnership: "Bill you won't be back in New York next year." So Bill returned to his second farm, which was in a beautiful setting, five miles outside of Kingston on the old Number Two highway, along the St. Lawrence River.

Yet the time came when he was to be called back to New York for his final big bow to Broadway. The year was 1968, and the ceremony was the opening of the New Madison Square Gardens. So on Sunday night, February 18, eighteen-thousand were on hand for Bill's last hurrah. The stands were filled with admirers from the Thirtys, and the applause was again deafening as Bill skated out on the ice and re-enacted the first goal that he had scored in the old Garden. So loud were the voices of his admirers that few heard the introduction: "Ladies and gentlemen, here's the greatest right-winger in Ranger history, the man that scored the first goal for the Rangers in their first game in the old Garden. A man that was instrumental in bringing the team two Stanley Cups. The leading scorer in the N.H.L. 1926, 1932, and 1933, and tied Charlie for the honour in 1934. All-star first team in 1930, 1931, and 1932, and all-star on second team, four times. The introduction ended with the words, "Let's hear it for ... " – but you couldn't hear a thing – the applause was so overwhelming. Thus came Bill's farewell to hockey, although he was to see New York and Broadway one more time.

Back in Kingston, he loved the freedom of farming, and being with his growing family and the great outdoors. Grey Manor, his big fourteen-room mansion, looked out over the St. Lawrence River, and you could see the American channel from the upstairs bedrooms. There were sometimes as many as forty milking cows on the farm, and the whole family enjoyed the wonderful setting. Talking about the place, Bill told me it was like reliving his other childhood dream – the dream of having a spread by the water, where he once again could feel the freedom and the elation of owning part of the great outdoors. He and Claire not only enjoyed the life of the farm, the swimming, fishing and other outdoor activities, but they also travelled extensively. Finally, when the children were all grown and had left, the two decided to move into Kingston, where they bought a small apartment complex and remained there until 1973, when Bill moved to his last address on Park Street.

"What would you change?" I asked him as I was gathering my papers to leave. "Nothing, he replied, "I had it all: a lovely wife, a loving family; I fulfilled my childhood dream to play with the best; I owned what was to me the most beautiful piece of Canada, the Grey Stone Manor on the St. Lawrence. I enjoyed the same things after my retirement from hockey as I loved as a child, fishing, hunting, hiking, swimming, the outdoors, and just watching nature and all its glories.

For several years, he continued to live alone in an apartment with a big, wide double window, looking down on the city he had always loved. Few of his old friends were left, and of course the two important women of his life, Claire, and his daughter Billie Marie, were no long with him. But the other three members of his family showed their love in every way they could, and their children meant everything to Bill. There was nothing in life he needed or wanted. There were times he would have liked to turn back the pages and live life over again. Not all of those pages were that pleasant: the war years, for example, when he watched many of his buddies die. He still could remember the bodies piled up like cordwood at Vimy Ridge, and the horses who drew the guns being disembowled before his eyes. He still would shiver, thinking of those wet cold trenches. The smell of death is not easily forgotten, nor is the shock of talking to a friend one moment only to look over and see him sitting dead on the toilet the next.

When he came to that time in his life, however, he would quickly flip the pages to reach the glory years in the Soo, Saskatoon, and New York. Then he would feel the deep satisfaction of knowing he had truly accomplished what he had set out in life to achieve. Perhaps the logo used by the great hockey mentor, Father Athol Murray, who founded Notre Dame College in Wilcox, Saskatchewan, says it best. Hanging over the hard-drinking old priest's former quarters are the words of St. Augustine of Hippo: "To him who does what within him lies, God will not deny his grace."

I did not get to visit Bunny, but Joe Fahey did. Bun was also slowing down a bit, with two bad hips, but Joe found him as jovial and happy-go-lucky as ever. I want him to know that he, too, was a hero to somebody else very close to me – and that was my brother, Pete, a priest, who died a couple of years ago, in Rome. It was Bun's bubble-gum card that my brother always carried, and it was his name he always took, when we played those shinny games on the street. Perhaps Pete made an early discovery about his hero – the quality of humility. All his life, Bun was overshadowed by Bill, and if there was ever a hockey player to display the great virtue of humility, it had to be Bun. In Bill's words, "He was a better hockey player and skater than I was, but he never got the credit." To me, those words expressed the love of one brother for another, but to Pete they were fundamental. Each of us sees his heroes differently. So I want Bun to know that he, too, is not forgotten.

During my visit, I had spoken to Bill about my book, and he had asked whom else I had written about. "An old friend of yours, Dollar Bill, the bootlegger," I replied. He smiled and said, "I'm in good company. I will never forget the Dollar diving into the cold Rideau waters, clothes, cap, and all, to retrieve a case of beer."

As we were about to leave, I asked Bill who he felt to be his closest friend. "Frankie Boucher," he replied, without hesitation, "and just before he passed away, Claire and I, and Bunny and his wife, went down to say goodbye." So there you have it, the answer of a real man. This was the Frank Boucher that Bill had insisted be brought to New York to centre with himself and Bun. This was the great centre who had become his constant companion, on and off the ice. This was the same Frankie that was to tell Bill in the Spring of '53, "I guess we won't need you back next year." "Winning's the name of the game you know," said Bill gazing toward the window, "and we were losers." Well, maybe winning is the name of the game on the ice, but loyalty and forgiving mark a man anywhere.

Walking down the hall from Bill's apartment Joe finally broke the silence when he turned and said, "He's quite a man." "Yes," I replied, as we stopped at the elevator, "but what is more important, at least to me, is that he is my kind of man and there are few of them left."

I had one more visit with Bill. It was the following year at Christmas time. He had moved from his apartment to the Providence Manor on Montreal Street, closer to the district where he had spent his childhood. By now, he needed nursing care. I brought him his bottle of brandy and he got out of bed and sat in a chair. I think he was in pain, but he hid it well. Pain was just another part of life for Bill, and he wanted to go out skating. "I was just thinking before you came in," he began, "that I'm getting a little lonely for Claire and Billy Marie and I hope to see them soon. There is one last thing I have to do, and that's to say goodbye to New York.

"They want me down there in January as they are having a special night for me. I don't really feel up to it, but it is something I have to do. Two of my sons, Jim and Murray, are going with me. But there is another fellow who should have been invited, my brother Bunny. I guess I once told you that I had been granted nearly everything I wished for in life, but I have one wish left – that Bunny will make it to the Hall of Fame. Surely there must be a place for a fellow of his calibre when there were so many enshrined who just talked their way in. It takes three players to make a line like we had in New York, and Bunny was as much a part of it as Franky and I.

"Just the other day, one Toronto writer wrote that Bunny was once flattened by King Clancy and I went to his rescue. Bunny could put Clancy in his hip pocket any day he wished, along with nearly any other player of the day. He was tough but underrated, and, believe me, he could look after himself. He was too good-natured, and never complained, so Franky and I always came out the heroes."

Well, Bill did make it to New York for the big occasion and it was a sell-out crowd. It was the first time the Alumni, four-hundred strong, had been allowed to pick the recipient. This time he walked slowly, rather than skated, as he had at his last hurrah, to centre ice. Although only a handful of the crowd ever saw him play, the applause was deafening, because the name "Cook" was still a legend around the Big Apple. Bill graciously accepted the award: a painting of Bill himself, scoring the first ever goal in Madison Gardens. For a moment he was young again, while the picture brought back memories. He stood in silence for a minute. Then he took a bow and, walking to the stand, he waved goodbye to New York for the very last time.

On May 6 1986, Joe Fahey's brother Jack, called and told me that Bill had passed away. Jack had been visiting his aunt in the same building, and he had gone up to see Bill the night before he died. "I guess he was in pain," said Jack, "but he hid it to the end. Yet right up to the last, I knew there was something bothering him. He kept repeating, 'Maybe someday, Bunny, you will get your dues.'"

I was unable to attend his funeral, but I met King Clancy, who died a few months later, and he told me all about it. I have, however, visited Bill's grave, just down from my brother's in St.Mary's Cemetery. There was no epitaph on his stone, but I knew that Granny Rice, a sports writer of Bill's era, had said it for him years ago:

> *When the one great scorer comes,*
> *To write against your name,*
> *He marks not what you won or lost,*
> *But how you played the game.*

My kind of people   **6**

Newspaper Days in Smiths Falls

Now, let's get back to the forties, with me out of college and working at my first job, which was digging culverts on the highway. My boss was Big Bill Harvey, of Harvey Construction. That lasted for seven months. By the summer of '48, I was up the Mountain Road north of the village of Westport, digging pole holes for the Hydro. I had started digging about a year previously and there was a line of poles half-way to Perth. On an average day, thanks to the foreman, "Short Ass Johnny," you would dig four holes, two feet across and six down.

On this particular day, "Slow" Joe McCann and I were taking a well-deserved rest, and we got to talking. Joe calculated that we had worked 252 days, and since we averaged twenty-four feet down each day, that we had penetrated Mother Earth some 6,000 feet, or well over a mile.

"If hell is down," says Joe, "we must be getting pretty close." That started me worrying, as things were bad enough already. So that night I packed it in, and the next morning I was in Smiths Falls, at the employment office, looking for a job. The only thing advertised was for a reporter at a place called Standard Press on Russell Street.

Now a pen would certainly be a lot lighter than a shovel, so it seemed a good idea to head down there right away. The owner and head push was a fellow named Jack Blackburn, formerly of the Windsor *Star*. Jack was pretty good as writers went, but never had enough time to get much of it done. He was rather a sour-looking fellow, with his head always cocked to one side, like a woodpecker peering in a knot hole.

He told me that he had just been appointed staff correspondent to the Ottawa *Citizen*, and was also a stringer for all three Toronto dailies. Along with this, he had a printing press, and ran off a lot of flyers and commercial printing. As a result of his work load, he was in need of a good leg-man who could write a little copy. During my interview Jack did not ask all that much, but then again he didn't usually talk all that much about anything. He told me to make myself comfortable, sit down at the typewriter, look out the window and, in a hundred words or less, knock off a little story about anything my eyes might behold. It just so happened that just as I was looking a well-dressed fellow was having a leak on the street across the way by McCaws dairy. Right off, I began with the words: "Well-dressed man, whom I presume is the Mayor, had taken advantage of his office to relieve himself on the street." Then I got down to a little more presuming. I suggested that, considering the size of the lake he left in front of him, he had consumed in the neighbourhood of thirteen beers. Finally, Jack snaps up the copy and begins to read. Now I never do remember Jack ever smiling, but a kind of crack appeared on one side of his face. "You're hired," he said.

Jack certainly did have his own brand of humour. I'd only been working for him about a month, when he suffered a heart-attack. So I went down to the hospital to see him. The head nurse told me it was nip and tuck for a while, but she thought the worst was over and I could go in and see him. "Somebody up there must like you, Jack," I say in the way of a greeting. "Like hell they do," says Jack. "Somebody up there don't want me."

Anyway, the day he hired me, he arranged room-and-board, up the street, at a lovely home run by a friend of his, Mrs. White. He also gave me a twenty to tide me over until pay day. Deciding I would need a little identification, he then went out to the shop and had his printer make up a press card, designating me as the sole staff correspondent of the *Plum Hollow Post* and stating (in fine print), that I should be allowed all the usual privileges accorded to the press.

My first assignment was to cover the town council meeting, which was to take place that night. But one of the many mistakes Jack made regarding myself was giving me that pay advance. I got as far as the Rideau Hotel and, with one thing and another, I didn't reach the town hall till around midnight. There was nobody left at the meeting when I arrived, except one young fellow sitting at a table doing a little writing. I walked up to him and introduced myself. I told him I was new in town and had had a hard time finding the place. He was quite sympathetic, and said something about it being a little hard to find the town hall, since most towns only have one. Then he told me he was Eddy Weese of the Ottawa *Journal*. We got to talking and he seemed a nice enough fellow. I told him I had a morning deadline, and needed to phone in a story by one a.m. to a rewrite man at the *Citizen*. He said, that's no problem, I could use *his* story as long as I changed the lead and the ending. Well, this was the beginning of a long and lasting relationship with my friend "Scoop" Weese.

We talked a bit more that night, and he told me he was a local boy who had grown up and got his schooling in the town. When I offered him a little snort, he began to lecture me a bit, stressing that it was solely for my own good. He explained that since we were in the newspaper business, we would be dealing with a lot of would-be pillars of the community, who had a lot of dust in their own closets, but liked to present a well-vacuumed image in public. He asked if I though I had a drinking problem. I assured him I didn't, and that the only problem I had was getting it at times.

Filling me in a little more on himself, he then said that he neither drank nor smoked, and was staying with an older cousin, a girl called Rosie, who was a stringer for the Kingston *Whig-Standard*. Thanking Eddy, after copying off his story, I headed up to the station to phone it in.

The next morning I was up early to get to the paper, and I must say the write-up was pretty good, thanks to Eddy, and the *Citizen* rewrite man. Right off, I decided this fellow Weese was an okay guy. We had arranged to meet at Durant's lunch counter at noon, and I was having a coffee there when in he walked. He congratulated me on my first story, and then started introducing me to the regulars.

There was the owner, Rusty Durant, who never missed a sporting event; Pete O'Brian, a baseball umpire and a walking encyclopedia, when it came to sports; and Ozzie Biggs, another sports authority, as well as being a partner of Pete's in the slot-machine business. The hand-shaking had just begun when who should walk in but the Hunter twins, Dibb and Debb. Now these two were a legend around Smiths Falls during the fifties. They ran a delivery service that had a real personal touch. Everything was delivered on foot, and, whether it be a priority letter or a flyer, the "Flying Brothers" guaranteed delivery. Now there were some who said that their service only surpassed the post office by a couple of days, but O'Brian claimed you could always depend on a third-day service.

When the brothers appeared each morning at the lunch room, they had a greeting of their own. For O'Brian, Biggs, and anyone they liked, it was the palms-down sign, with the words, "You're safe." For strangers, or anyone they didn't exactly trust, it was a thumbs-up sign, "You're out." On this particular morning, they notified all that they could not hang around too long, as they had some door-to-door flyers they had to get out for the Beamish store down the street, which was having a sale. Just before they were leaving, Durant told them not to forget to be back at seven that evening to set up pins in his bowling alley. They both gave him the "out" sign, and told him they were no longer going to set up pins. Apparently, some fellow by the name of Jog Crate let a practice ball go the other night, and it almost beheaded them both. "So get yourself another boy," said Debb. "You're *out!*"

The place was gradually filling up: Reg Wride, the chief of police; Eddy Fagan, the fire chief; Frank Hogan, the sign painter and sports promoter; and a fellow named Barry Stevens, whom Eddy introduced as a reporter on the local paper, the *Record News*. It seems Barry had been one of those big city men with the Ottawa *Journal*, who had somehow ended up in Smiths Falls. He was an aloof kind of fellow, none too friendly, but he greeted me cordially enough.

Well, after all the greeting I asked Eddy what was on his blotter today. He said he would check around at the police station; have a free dinner down at the Rotary Club meeting; and, if he got anything worthwhile, he'd see me back here about six. So I congratulated him on last night's story, and told him I would really appreciate it if I might use his stuff till I got a little better acquainted with the town. He assured me he would look after things.

After leaving Durant's, I thought I would visit the Lee Hotel, which I'd heard a lot about. I did not have much in the way of an entrance fee, only a couple of bucks, left over from Jack's twenty, but it just happened to be c.p.r. payday and, as it turned out, I did not need much. If you have ever been in a railway town on payday, you'll know where that saying "millionaire for a day" comes from. Everybody was buying, and I managed to meet a lot of new faces and have a very pleasant afternoon.

Come six o'clock, I headed back down to Durant's, and Weese gave me a few little items: a report on the Rotary meeting; a write-up by his cousin Rosie, on a meeting of the Women's Institute; and also an account of an accident. He explained that this last item was particularly important, because there was more to it than met the eye. It seems that the beautiful daughter of a prominent family had been injured in a car-crash, while in the company of a married man. Eddie and Rosie's paper would certainly want a picture of this young lady. Eddie assured me he would try to come up with one himself, but, if he couldn't, he might have to use my services. In the mean-time there was a hockey match that night between Pembroke and the locals, and he would appreciate it if I covered for both of us. He then went on to say that Hal Dewey, the team coach, was sitting just across the way, and he would introduce me. Hal, after I met him, said he would look after things, and I should just come round to meet him in the dressing-room, after the game.

The locals won the game 3-2, and, true to his word, Hal had a nice little write-up ready for me, summary and all. I met "Scoop" after the game and presented him with the story. I also told him that I was meeting a lot of interesting people, and getting a lot of gossip about some of these "pillars of society" he had been telling me about. He said it was important I remember anything real juicy, as we could always use it, one way or another, later on. He also said that he had had no luck getting the picture, and wondered if I would give it a try.

He gave me the address of the girl's aunt, a rather elderly spinster and quite religious. Telling me to make sure I called on her before I made the rounds of the hotels, Scoop left to cover a Board of Education meeting. So the next morning I was up bright and early, dressed in my best, and knocking at the good lady's door. I told her who I was and how touched I had been by the tragedy. I went on to say that I heard a fellow named Weese, from the Ottawa *Journal*, had been there the day before. I warned her to not have any truck with the likes of him, or with that Barry Stevens, who worked for the local paper. All reporters are the same, I warned her, they just look for the sensational in order to sell papers. As for myself, I was just biding my time till I made enough money to put myself through Bible College. I then went on to say that I was a member of her church, and had been impressed by the devoutness of the poor girl and her parents. Well, the good woman gives me a lovely photo, and tells me to return it at the Presbyterian church Sunday service, down the street.

As you can imagine, Weese was more than happy when I presented him with the picture, and he got a copy run off at Hy Fund's Studio. Sunday morning, I was at the Presbyterian church, dressed to kill, and I even walked up and shook hands with the minister, Mr. Latimore. Well, it looked like a happy ending. The girl recovered, married a nice guy, and, I take it, lived happily ever after. But next day I went down to the Russell Hotel, and met an old ball-player named Lefty Muldoon. In the way of a greeting he says, "I hear you even get drunk on Sunday," "How's that?" I asked. "Well," he went on, "it's all over town that yesterday you got into the wrong church."

After the picture episode, Weese did not ask me to do all that much, only the odd sporting event. Then one day he decided that it might look a little better if I turned up at a few local functions. He suggested I might begin the next morning, when they would be holding court. I never had liked going to court, although I had made the odd appearance over the years. But, to please Weese, I figured I'd better oblige, so I got down there and sat through a couple of cases. Then the magistrate said the next case was to be held *in camera*, and only authorized individuals could remain. I got up to go, but Weese told me to sit down again, so I was forced to linger. The case involved a vacuum salesman who was accused of assaulting a married woman. On and on it went, and finally the woman took the stand. The lawyer asked her if she was sure the accused penetrated her. The poor woman was forced to admit she wasn't quite sure, as she was eight months pregnant and it was a little hard to tell. Well, for some reason or other, that started me laughing and after a few minutes the magistrate said we'd better take a short recess. When we got outside Weese told me that maybe it would be better if I didn't go back in. He added it might be better still if I stayed away from court altogether. So I was excused from that duty as well.

Now, the only occasion I found the time to see my boss, Jack, was on pay-day, and then only for a minute or so. He told me I was doing a good job and added that he had noticed Weese and I used the same writing style. He also told me that if anything should break within a twenty-mile radius of the town, I should feel free to get a driver and pay him the going rate. As it turned out, a lot of little things *did* come up outside the town, so I engaged several drivers, but none were too dependable until I met up with a guy named Don Mc-Kenney. He was a clean-cut young fellow, active in sports, and up every morning at four a.m., to deliver milk for his father's dairy. His route included an early morning trip to Merrickville. Now, since I was getting a little flak from my landlady about the hours I was keeping, and since Don was going to work when I was coming home, I started just piling myself into the truck, where I slept while he did his deliveries.

A few years later Don was to achieve his boyhood dream when he played his first game for the Boston Bruins in 1954. He again performed in style in 1960, winning the Lady Byng trophy in Boston. Two years after that he was traded to Toronto, where he helped his team win the Stanley Cup. After stops in Detroit and St. Louis, he retired in 1969, when his legs had finally had enough. Just last winter, "Loop" Montgomery and I ran into him at a high-school hockey tournament in Toronto. He told us he was now coaching down in Boston, at Northeastern University, with his old Boston teammate, Ferny Flaman. He was in town, he said, to watch the tournament and scout for talented kids looking for a scholarship to help further their education. He also told us he was just a couple of subjects away from obtaining his own degree. Not bad, for a fellow who dropped out of school in grade ten to help his invalid father run the family business.

Even now, with a driver and all, I began to feel that I was not pulling my weight when it came to my friend Weese. So I decided I would tell him about this really big project I was working on. I explained I had started to write a book. It was to be called "The Way it Is," and was about Smiths Falls and the surrounding district. I showed him all the bits and pieces of information I'd been gathering, and went on to say that just as he had been ghosting for me, I would be ghosting for him. Thus, when the book was finished, the author would be duly recorded as none other that "Edward Weese." Then I began to ask a few questions, like, if he knew how many bootleggers were operating in the district; how many unsolved murders had taken place in the last ten years; and how come the town was often referred to as "Little Chicago?" I could see right away that I was holding his interest, but he was a true-blue native, and soon began to have doubts about disclosing anything detrimental regarding his home town. So I finally did not give him any particulars, just as I don't intend to give any to you.

The truth is, I really can't say anything offensive about the towns in the Valley. Somehow or other, it always seems that one of my old friends is getting elected for some important office – people like Tom Sullivan in Arnprior, Ben Franklin in Nepean, and Ducks Lee in the Falls. I should add that my motives are not entirely concerned with loyalty. Those fellows could also tell a lot about me that I wouldn't want to be generally known.

So I dropped the idea of the book for the time being, and Weese and I continued to operate in the same old way. Now, every so often, he would take a day or two off, leaving me in charge. So one warm Sunday in July, he decided he needed a day of rest, and, since Sundays were usually pretty quiet, he thought he would be safe in leaving me to handle things. It was indeed quiet. I sat in the park for most of the afternoon and evening, visiting with passersby, until about ten p.m.

Then along comes "Jake the Rake," who had also done some chauffering for me in the past, although it had not worked out too well. There had been a bad accident in Franktown, and Jake and I had been on our way there when the two of us got stranded beneath the low railway bridge, coming onto the Carleton road. Jake was driving a truck, and he had forgotten to take off the high racks. So there we sat, wedged beneath the bridge, with traffic stopped in every direction.

Along comes one of the town cops, a fellow named "Smart Ass" Charlie. "How the hell did you fellows get stuck under there?" he shouts. "We ain't stuck," says Jake. "I was just trying to move the bridge and it's stuck." Well, needless to say, we caused quite a lot of bad feeling. Also needless to say, we didn't get to Franktown.

This Sunday evening, however, Jake was in better shape. He informed me that three people had been drowned in Big Rideau Lake at Portland, and one of them was my friend, the Indian guide, Billy Lake. So Jake tells me he can certainly get me there, and this time things will be different because his friend "Connors," who had a cab business up the street will let us use one of his cars. It was a habit of Connors that when he was a little under the weather himself, he would sleep it off on the couch in his office, leaving the keys in one of the cars, with a note in the glove compartment which said, "Help yourself, but please leave the fare."

So Jake and I piled in the car and headed for Portland, and when we came to the first stop sign, he slammed on the brakes and out pop two full bottles of rye from underneath the seat. It was a custom in those days for all cab companies to keep a little booze in stock, to take care of after-hour and Sunday emergencies.

Anyhow, we got to Portland, rented a boat, had a few shots, and reached the scene of the disaster, where I obtained all the particulars. By the time we returned to shore it was pretty late, and I told Jake I didn't see how I could get this story in for the morning *Citizen*. Well, Jake looked across the lake, "There's a light on that cottage over there," he says, "Why don't you go over, and you can ask if we can use his phone."

So I stuck one of the jugs in my back pocket, and over we went. I rapped at the door, and a tall, rather stern-looking fellow let me in. I explained my predicament and he let me use the phone. But just as I was about to leave, stuffing the papers into my pocket, the jug fell out and broke. The fellow took my arm and kind of hurried me outside. Well, once we were back in the car, Jake applied the brakes again at the first stop sign, and out came another bottle.

So everything was okay. When he had returned the cab, we went back to the park and finished the bottle. Then we both decided to retire for the night. I left a message beside my bed for me to call the *Journal*, for Eddy, first thing in the morning. Well, I must have been really fatigued, because I did not come to till the afternoon of the next day. The landlady was pounding on my door. "You're wanted on the phone!" she yelled. I went down to answer it, and my friend and boss, Jack, was at the other end of the line. He tells me all hell has broken loose. The *Journal* has a big story on a drowning in Portland, and we have nothing. But that was not the worst part of it. The really bad part was that the fellow who covered the story (which was me), was supposed to be representing the *Citizen*, but he had phoned in the story to the wrong paper, and he was using the phone which belonged to none other than the *Citizen's* publisher. Mr. Southam was also known to be a bit intolerant when it came to alcohol.

Well, I go back to my room, tear up the message I had left myself, and head down to see Jack. He said he thinks it's only a matter of time before we would be severing our relations with the Ottawa daily. Our only chance to keep going – at least with me on the payroll – was to start our own paper. He explained that it would be a four-page free sheet: one page of newsy little stories, and the rest filled up with advertising. He said he thought he could handle one page of advertising if I did the writing and looked after the other two.

So we came out with our new paper. *The Post* (not the *Plum Hollow Post*, as we never got any advertising from there). For the first edition, I achieved two full-page ads from two different breweries: one from Molsons, who were represented in the district by Gordy Morley, and one from Tommy Monaghan, the Labatts representative. Since I was known to both as a good customer, I had no trouble talking them into buying the space. The only problem was that I promised each of them that their ad would appear on the front page. When the paper came out, it was Labatts that graced the front page. I had a hard time explaining to Morley that, since the pages were not numbered, it shouldn't make any difference if *his* ad was front or back. It all depended on how he picked up the paper. Jack had had a harder time coming up with his full page, but did manage to obtain ten small ads.

Things went pretty well for the first couple of months, and the paper was beginning to look like a going concern. We had it delivered, door-to-door, by the "Flying Brothers," Dibb and Debb, to about a thousand homes. But we made one big mistake: we tried to cut down the brothers' regular price of ten dollars a thousand, so we were in their bad books right from the start.

When Jack decided that we should branch out, and publish a couple of thousand more, to be sent to the various rural villages, we were surprised when they said they would take that contract too. It was not long before we were to find out why.

One day "Molson" Morley was crossing the bridge at the foot of Beckwith street, when he sees Dibb and Debb, weighted down with papers. He stopped and watched as they dumped a bundle into the water, first on the east side of the bridge, and then on the west.

Finally he walked up and asked what they were doing. "We're sending that cheap bastard of a Murphy's paper to Portland and Merrickville by water," was the reply. Well, Gord asked if they were sure that the water would flow both ways. They replied firmly that it did, their old public school geography teacher had told them so.

Of course the story got around, and the next week Jack was unable to come up with any advertising at all, so the paper went out with one blank page. Tommy and Morley did not seem to mind, but the bad publicity did us in and, finally, the paper folded. A day or so after its passing, Jack asked me if I had any plans. When I replied in the negative he said he had one for me. He told me he had a cousin in Vancouver who owned a weekly, and was in need of a reporter. That said, he handed me an envelope with a hundred dollars and a one-way ticket to Vancouver. I took the money, but handed back the ticket, telling him that if things did not work out I might be stuck in the West. "That," said Jack, "was my plan."

Well, it was years later, when I was living in Toronto, that I finally understood was Jack had meant. I heard that my friend Weese had been appointed editor of the Smiths Falls paper, so I gave him a call to tell him I had finished *his* book. I knew right away by the sound of his voice he was not too interested. He told me that my friend Jack had passed away the week before, and he had got down to see him just before his death. Somehow, he went on, my name came up, and Jack, weak as he was, said, "That Murphy shortened my life by some twenty years, but a fellow has to die of something."

Weese went on to say his own life had taken a turn for the better since my departure from that neck of the woods, and he would like to keep it that way. Before hanging up the phone he added, "And good luck with *your* book!"

I would like to be able to say that, after I left the paper, the world unfolded as it should, and I went on to make it big in the newspaper business. But such was not the case. A month or so later, I was back where I started a little over two years previously. This time, I had traded my pen for another shovel, and on March 17, 1951, I was making my way north to Chalk River, hand-bombing an old steam locomotive, No. 3518. It was a long while before I took up the pen again, but in the next ten years I shovelled my share of coal.

The Almonte Wreck

I hope you will allow me to get a little more serious for one chapter, as I tell you the story of the Almonte wreck. During my ten years of railroading I was to hear of many tragedies, related by veteran railroaders, but nothing to compare with the Almonte crash. It was the biggest in the history of Eastern Ontario railroading.

Little do people realize the complexities involved in railroading, and the many factors that can be involved in such a tragedy. Too often, the blame has been placed on human error, with not enough consideration given to other factors.

Today, due to the introduction of the block system, with its warning lights, railroading is safer, and far less complicated. Even now, however, there are instances where human error is not the contributory factor.

I was to railroad with many of those who survived the Almonte wreck, and we seldom passed through the little town without some mention of that terrible tragedy. It has always been my personal belief that the engineer of the troop train, Bill Richardson, got a raw deal when the cards were shuffled and placed face-up in front of the coroner's jury, even though they finally absolved him of blame. By relating the story that follows, I will let you, the reader, decide for yourself.

As Engine 2802 rounded the curve, just north of the town of Almonte, fireman Sammy Thompson shouted, "Clear board!" Then as the engine passed the mile board and crossed the steel trestle, hissing its way through the mist coming off the Mississippi River he yelled again – this time frantically, "Plug her!" – It was too late. Although engineer Bill Richardson heard the anguished warning, and slammed the throttle closed as he threw the automatic brake into the emergency "big hole," the giant engine screeched onward. When it finally came to a stop it had plowed through three wooden coaches of Local 550, standing at the Almonte station, loading passengers.

All hell broke loose in the Valley as the terrific crash shook the houses in every direction. The earth shivered, and then for a moment there was silence, followed by terrified screams from the men, women, and children trapped in the wreck.

The tragedy that followed went on record as the second worst wreck in the history of Canadian railroading, with the final count being thirty-six dead and 150 injured.

Confusion reigned throughout the little town until people realized what had happened. Then, suddenly, hundreds of residents began to appear from the darkness through the cascades of rain that pelted down from the pitch-black sky.

It was just two days after Christmas on December 27, 1941. Hundreds of Valley residents, loaded down with presents, were returning to their jobs in Ottawa after spending the joyous holiday with their families and loved ones. The Local 550 and Engine 2518 were as much a part of the Valley as the little towns and villages along the single, winding track which snaked its way north from Ottawa to Chalk River. It was wartime, and for most people of the Valley the train was their only means of transport.

It had been a mild winter day, with soft snow falling, clinging to the trees, presenting a Christmas-card atmosphere along the shimmering line of steel. Visibility was poor. As the hours passed, the snow had changed to sleet, and later to rain.

For the crew of Local 550, it had begun as just another work day when they left Petawawa Station, to make their way south towards Ottawa. The engineer, Joe Sauve, had made the trip hundreds of times, and knew the run like the back of his hand. The same held true for the conductor, M.O. O'Connel, and his assistant, Jack Morris, along with the two trainmen, Joe Tunney and Tom Gilmour. Frank Dixon, the fireman, was also a veteran railroader.

For the crew of the troop train, which was pulled by Engine 2802, the situation was different. It had been just twenty-one days since the "hogger," Bill Richardson, was set up as an engineer. Most of his railroad career had been confined to freight. Sammy Thompson, the fireman, was making his first trip on a passenger train and was still a rookie, having railroaded for only a year and a half. Jack Howard, the conductor, was a veteran railroader, but had worked mostly on freight trains, as had his regular brakeman, Had Rowe. The other brakeman, Gordon Smith, was making his first trip on a passenger train, having just begun his railway career.

Before leaving Chalk River, Smith had lamented to conductor Howard that he had no uniform to wear back on the "varnished" (the railroad term for a passenger train). Jack, a good-natured man, laughingly told him, "Don't worry, wear mine. You'll look good in the brass and I won't need it." Ironically, that statement became a fact. Howard was never to wear the uniform again.

Local 550 had left Petawawa on time, with twelve coaches and all the tonnage 2518 could pull. Since it was holiday time, every coach would be filled before the train reached Almonte. After making several stops along the way, it began losing time. Frank Dixon, the fireman, had been fighting the old girl for more steam all along the route – gaining a bit as they stopped at the various stations to pick up passengers, but losing it again en route. Little old 2518 had a bad reputation of not steaming, as many a railroader could attest over the years. She was an ageing, cantankerous hog if there ever was one, and she gave me many a hard trip when I was a railroader.

After leaving Renfrew, things worsened. Even though it was all downhill to Arnprior, she continued to lose time. The troop train was running behind her, its white flags flapping in the breeze (which denoted it as an Extra, with no right-of-way). It was on a faster schedule than the first-class Local – and was gradually bearing down. Somehow, with the sixth sense that many old-time railroaders seem to develop, Richardson warned his fireman to be on a sharp lookout for the train ahead. "You never know about the 2518," he cautions, "the old bastard may not be steaming." Although the weather was bad, both Richardson and his fireman kept their heads out of the cab windows, braving the wind and the blinding sleet.

It was not until they had reached Renfrew that they stopped for orders – in writing – notifying them that Local 550 was indeed in trouble and running behind schedule. The orders specified that they must remain there for twenty minutes, so Thomson took on coal and water. After twenty minutes had elapsed they pulled out and headed cautiously towards Arnprior – again keeping a sharp lookout for the train ahead, but trying to maintain the schedule set down in their running orders.

At 8:01 p.m. the troop train pulled into Arnprior, and the order board was again on. The clearance time on the orders read 8:15, so the troop train was once more held up. This time for fourteen minutes. When the time had elapsed Richardson got two blasts on the communication cord from the conductor. He immediately thought that the orders were being changed again, and that they would now be held at Arnprior until Local 550 left Almonte. Such was not the case. He was given a highball (the all-clear signal), and off they went. Richardson still continued cautiously, trying to maintain his running orders speed, but feeling a little uneasy about the train ahead. When he reached Pakenham, however, the order board was clear. Both he and his fireman felt a little more relaxed. Surely, they both thought, Local 550 must have cleared Almonte by now, or the board would be on, and they would be stopped. Regardless, he still eased her off as they went through Pakenham, and reminded Sammy to keep a sharp lookout for the board at Almonte – since the curve there was such that the fireman could see the board, mounted at the top of the old stone station, long before the engineer. As a result, when they rounded the curve coming into Almonte, Thompson put his head out of the cab window and saw that the board was green – or "clear," as it's known to railroadmen. Once again, Bill eased off the throttle and touched up the brake as he rounded the curve. But when the engine came into the straight both men were almost paralysed by what lay ahead. Their headlight picked up the taillights of Local 550. Horrified, Richardson immediately shut off the throttle and threw the brakes in emergency. But they were by now only a few cars from the standing train and both men knew the inevitable was about to happen.

Minutes later, the railway line at the station was in shambles. The three tail-end coaches of the Local were piled up like splintered lumber. How anyone was rescued alive remains a mystery to this day. Yet hundreds climbed out of wrecked coaches unassisted. The steel rails were ripped away from the ties and slung along the station platform.

Following the wreck, the injured and the dead were taken to a variety of places within the town. The residents opened wide their doors, offering everything they could in the way of assistance. Inspector T.W. Cousins, of the Ontario Provincial Police, ordered all bodies to be brought to the old stone town hall, directly across from the station, where a temporary morgue was set up. Every commercial vehicle in town was volunteered and used as an ambulance to transport the dead and injured.

Throughout the night, relatives from all parts of the Valley streamed into the temporary morgue, as news of the wreck spread across the countryside. Under the supervision of Provincial Police, rows of blankets were turned down, as people tried to recognize friends and relatives.

Almost as if they had anticipated such a tragedy, the townspeople turned out to work through the night with the St. John's Ambulance, the Red Cross, and the soldiers and servicemen from both trains. So crowded was the little Almonte hospital that coal bins were being used as beds. The old O'Brien Theatre was turned into a first-aid station, and stores on the town's two main streets – Mill and Bridge – were also opened. Beds, taken from many of them, were used as stretchers. A special ambulance train was dispatched to the scene, made up of two sections, to bring some of the dead and injured to Ottawa. Once there, it required nearly two hours to get all the injured off the train, because it was almost impossible to get the make-shift stretchers through the narrow doors of the old coaches. There were eighty-six stretcher cases put aboard at Almonte, but three of the injured died on the train.

Most of the fatalities came from the Valley towns and villages: Killaloe, Barrys Bay, Pembroke, Cobden, and Renfrew. Minor operations were performed on the train, en route to Ottawa, with the patients being administered ether and narcotics.

Big 2802, although badly injured herself, was able to supply steam to those cars of the Local not demolished in the wreck, so that the rescuers could warm their wet, freezing hands. A large bonfire was lighted from the wreckage to illuminate the scene, so the workers could see to operate the large cranes. The wreck completely blocked the single-track line, and it took nearly two hours before the last person was gently hoisted from the tangled mess of wood and steel. Joe Johnson, one of the civilians who had answered the call, rescued twelve people himself. He said it was midnight when he pulled the last survivor from the wreck.

Perhaps the saddest sight of all was the body of a little three-year-old from Ottawa, dressed in a blue snow suit and wearing white snow boots, lying in the débris beside his father, who had also died in the wreck.

Almost immediately, c.p.r. officials, along with officials of the Department of Transport, began an investigation. The wreck had been the worst in Canada since 1910, when forty-three persons lost their lives in a derailment at the Spanish River Bridge, in Webbwood. The Attorney General's Department in Toronto also began an immediate investigation, led by the Chief Coroner of the time, Dr. Smirle Lawson. An inquest was scheduled for 7 January.

On the eve of the inquest, another tragedy occurred when Jack Howard, the conductor of the troop train, ended his life in the Rideau River at Smiths Falls. Howard had joined the c.p.r. as a porter at Smiths Falls in 1906, and became a brakeman two years later. He had been a conductor since 1911, and had one year to go for his pension. His body was found wedged among some logs, about one hundred yards below the dam.

Jack left behind a note to his son, all of which was never divulged to the public, but which was later read, in part, by members of the coroner's jury. It said that he was sorry that he had to take his own life, but he couldn't see anything else for it. He felt that he was in no way to blame for the wreck, but did not want to go to jail. Then he bade his son goodbye, and gave him some instructions on personal matters.

The inquest began as scheduled in the quaint stone town hall that had housed the dead and injured. Legal, medical, military and transportation officials, together with thirty witnesses from all walks of life, gathered to determine the cause of the disaster. Albert Ashfield, the long-time caretaker of the hall, worked strenuously throughout the morning, preparing the large auditorium on the second floor of the building. A green curtain was drawn across the stage, and the furniture of the room was arranged in a similar manner to a county court. Long rows of benches were set up for the hundreds of spectators, anxious to hear every word of evidence which might throw some light on the tragedy.

The tension was heightened by an announcement from the Premier of Ontario, who was also the Attorney General, that the inquiry would be wide open. No one would be spared during the process of determining the cause of the disaster.

Acting under these instructions, C.L. Snyder, Assistant Attorney-General, Dr. Smirle Lawson, Chief Coroner for the province, and W.W. Pollack, Crown Attorney for the County of Lanark, along with the coroner of the county, Dr. A.A. Metcalfe, convened in the morning to plan the inquest. A coroner's jury was formed, made up of G.W. Dunlop, Robert J. Neil, James Cochrane, E.J. Lee, and N.S. Lee, with Dunlop appointed foreman.

Canadian Pacific set up two special telegraph lines to handle the flow of reports, as newsmen gathered from Ottawa, Toronto, and Montreal. A temporary new headquarters was established in the freight sheds near the station – within one hundred yards of the crash. Most of the railway men, along with the witnesses called to testify, were housed in railway coaches parked in front of the station, across from the town hall.

The Almonte Hotel, the only hostelry then operating in town, was the headquarters for most of the officials attending the inquest. Bill Whitton, the manager was swamped by demands for accommodation. In some cases, reservations made several days previously had to be ignored. People were forced to canvass the entire town for accommodation, and eventually had to turn to private homes for shelter.

Upon their arrival, Dr. Lawson, C.L. Snyder, and Mr. Roebuck, and their out-of-town officials, gathered at the scene of the wreck. They stood on the tracks at the Main Street crossing, surveying the site, trying to visualize what occurred on the night of December 27. Police Chief William Peacock, who was standing on the station platform beside the ill-fated Local when it was struck, reconstructed the event as he remembered it.

The inquest began in the afternoon, with a detailed inquiry on the death of one, Frank White, of Eastview. Since he was a typical victim of the wreck, the jury's findings concerning the circumstances surrounding his death would apply to all victims of the catastrophe.

The first railroader to be called was the fireman of the troop train, Sammy Thompson. Cecil Snyder, the Assistant Attorney General, cross-examined Thompson, beginning with his railroad experience and proceeding to what happened on the night of the wreck. Thompson testified that he had had the best opportunity of seeing the green board at Almonte. He went on to say that the board at Pakenham, nine miles from Almonte, had also been green, and that the train was travelling about forty-five miles per hour between Arnprior and Almonte.

"What did you see when you rounded the curve coming into Almonte," asked Dr. Lawson. "I saw a clear board,"replied Thompson. "If you saw a clear board, the Chief Coroner asked, "did you presume that the Local was at the station in Almonte, or that it had reached Carleton Place?" "I presumed it had reached Carleton Place," was the reply. "You would have expected a danger signal had the Local still been at Almonte?" "Yes" Thompson replied.

Dr. Lawson: "If there had been a danger signal, or an automatic signal a mile out from the station, would you have stopped?"

"Yes, and the accident would have been avoided."

The next witness was engineer Bill Richardson, who explained this had been his first run as an engineer on a passenger train, since he had been set up as an engineer only twenty-one days before the wreck. He went on to say that although he had thirty-two years service as a railroader, most of it had been spent on freight trains.

"You knew that the Local was ahead of you?," asked Assistant Attorney General Snyder.

"Yes. I approached Pakenham cautiously, as I thought the Pakenham operator would have blocked me, but the signal was green. There was no sign of the Local. Approaching Almonte I eased off the throttle, and drifted for about two hundred feet before the brakes began to take hold. I let the train ride the brakes until I slowed down to about twenty-five miles an hour.

"I told my fireman to keep a sharp lookout when we came around the curve coming into Almonte, and he shouted 'Clear board,' which indicated to me that the Local had reached Carleton Place."

Mr. Snyder: "The green board indicated that the Local was either at Carleton Place or standing at the station in Almonte."

Richardson: "I had the right to believe that there would be a flare or some other warning if the train was still in Almonte."

"In your opinion," interjected Arthur Roebuck, council for the

Brotherhood of Engineers, "as an experienced railway man, is it in the interest of safety to leave this board green when a train is standing at the station?" "No," replied Richardson, "It might work better if the signal was changed to red if the train was standing at the station."

The engineer's answer would later change a certain rule in the *Rule Book*, that the bible of all railway men. The book is drawn up by the railway and submitted to the Board for approval – the same Board now called in to investigate the wreck. To this day, railroaders are still wondering how such a body could have been so lax as to approve that rule, which might never have been changed if the Almonte disaster had not occurred.

Railroaders were not alone in their condemnation. As Dr. Smirle Lawson immediately commented, "The cobwebs should be dusted off the rule books for the safety of all concerned."

Every crew member of the two trains, along with some thirty witnesses, were to testify during the inquest, and none directed any criticism at the members of the crew. This was to change, however, when the Superintendent of the Smiths Falls Division took the stand. He stated that the troop train should have disregarded its twenty-minute-late running order from Arnprior to Almonte, and followed the running order of the Local. Mr. Snyder asked, "Why did you say it was the fault of the troop train?" The Superintendent replied, "I did not say it was the fault of the troop train. I said that they exceeded the speed of train 550."

This testimony did not sway Coroner Lawson, even when the Superintendent was called to the stand and repeated this statement. In his summary to the jury, the coroner pointed out that it must not be overlooked that the original train order handed to engineer Richardson, called for a fast schedule, faster in places, than the speed of the Transcontinental Limited.

Thus, at the very beginning of this run, Richardson knew he was expected to make an especially fast time. But despite this request for fast time, it was now being sworn that it was the duty of the engineer to disregard his order, and follow along behind the Local at a speed no greater than that which the Local was travelling.

To me, these contradictory instructions for the operation of a train seem designed to confuse any man. In addition to interpreting conflicting instructions, he had to handle the big engine, estimate his speed, watch for signals, safeguard the lives of all the Canadian troops behind him, and also attempt to safeguard his own life and that of his crew.

He had also been given no warning that the Local in front of him was losing more and more time. He was reassured at Pakenham by the "all clear" green board. When he rounded the curve coming into Almonte he was reassured once again, by a second green board.

So, he brought his heavy train to Almonte two minutes ahead of the time the Local should have arrived, but actually twelve minutes late, according to his original "fast schedule." It may be that, because of the complicated rules, he was two minutes ahead of time: but it must be remembered that a first-class train, such as the Local, is allowed to arrive at a station five minutes ahead of time!

In summing up his evidence to the jury Dr. Lawson stated: "It seems to me that we're living in a new era. We have changed from peacetime to wartime, with increased traffic on the railroad.

"The efficient man of today is the man who can interpret the age and the times in which he is living, and see that the necessary safety devices are erected to ensure the welfare of the public, before such a calamity occurs and makes it necessary to hold an inquest such as this.

"Nothing should be left undone to ensure the safety of our citizens and our armed forces, who must be conveyed on our railways in these times of great emergency to our nation.

"It is for you the jury to decide how Frank White came to his death, what was the cause and manner of his death, and to make any recommendations which will prevent a future similar accident."

The jury deliberated for three hours, then handed down their decision late on the Saturday afternoon of January 10.

"We the coroner's jury, appointed by you to inquire where, how, and by what means the late Frank White came to his death, beg leave to report as follows:

"It is our finding that the blame for this wreck must be placed entirely on the Canadian Pacific Railway Company for three reasons:

"First, they had no operator stationed at Pakenham when, in our opinion, the accident might have been avoided by a twenty-minute block system.

"Second, there was no protective signal at the most dangerous curve at the entrance of the town of Almonte.

"Third, the green light showing above the Almonte station gave the engineer of the 2802 the impression he might proceed. Had this signal been red, according to the testimony of the engineer and the fireman, the train could have been stopped." The jury then went on to say that they placed no blame whatever on either of the crews, but did feel that an effort could have been made from Smiths Falls to call the operator at Pakenham, who lived in the station.

In their concluding statement, the jury recommended the following safeguards in order to prevent the occurrence of another tragedy:

1 That an operator be placed on steady duty at Pakenham.
2 That an automatic station protection signal should be immediately installed at Almonte.
3 That a standing order be issued for a speed limit not exceeding twenty-five miles per hour through Almonte, and that this order be strictly enforced by railway officials.
4 That the block signal device at Almonte station be changed, to give protection to standing trains.

Perhaps the part of the verdict that touched many railwaymen and spectators the most was the exoneration of the conductor, Jack Howard. When the hearing of the evidence had been completed, jury foreman, G.W. Dunlop, asked that the jury be allowed to read the message Howard had left to his son. Dr. Lawson complied with their wish, explaining however that there were certain personal references which he did not intend to read to the public.

James Maloney, a well-known lawyer from Arnprior, who represented a number of passengers involved in the wreck, praised the way the investigation was carried out. "I think Ontario is extremely fortunate in having such capable and honourable officials. They have thrown the inquiry wide open, so that all possible evidence could be brought before the public. There had been the impression that efforts were being made to cover up the unfortunate tragedy, but such was not the case."

Most of the people who had attended the trial left the little town of Almonte that wintry Saturday, believing that the end of the inquest would close the books on the Almonte wreck. Such was not the case. All disasters where the military are involved remain open. There are still, it seems, questions that were never answered or asked.

One question which still baffles railwaymen is why the man in charge was allowed to continue in his capacity as head of a railway division which a coroner's jury had found to possess unsafe conditions.

This was the same boss who, after the inquest, banished engineer Bill Richardson from the main line. Richardson was to spend his last days working on the end of a shovel in Prescott yard. His banishment also stipulated that he would receive no pension.

The last time I saw Bill in Prescott I told him I was doing a story on the Almonte wreck. He remained silent for what seemed an hour then he said, "Come back some time when I have shovelled my last ton of coal. I may have an end for your story."

I went back the following year, but I was too late. Bill had joined his old conductor friend, Jack Howard. Somehow I am glad now that I never got around to that final meeting, although I would have liked to have said goodbye. Anyway, "Railway men don't talk!" so it's better left that way.

I am sure both Bill and Jack have passed that other jury – like the one that exonerated them both so many years ago in Almonte. If there are any trains in the great beyond, I know they will both be riding first class. They paid their dues.

My kind of people

8

Cowboy Curran

Years ago, when the swallows got together to say goodbye before heading south, lining the telephone wires for miles, you got the feeling fall was setting in. Sure enough, a few days later signs would be posted around the community, advertising the numerous fall fairs in the area.

Delta was the first, followed by Lansdowne, Lombardy, and finally the big extravaganza: Kingston. Every fair had it's merry-go-round, ferris wheel, and roller-coaster, and you could smell the french fries and the cotton candy a mile before you reached the grounds. To me as a child the big attraction was the horse races. Each fair had it's little one-third-of-a-mile track, with tight turns, and a bit rough, to say the least. Today, you see bigger tracks than that designed for humans at the various athletic schools. It is little wonder that Eastern Ontario was the breeding ground for some of Canada's greatest harness-racing drivers. To drive on some of those fairground tracks was like trying to thread a needle with your eyes closed.

At Delta and Lansdowne, the presiding judge, starter and chief official, was Hilt "The Baliff" Emerson. Hilt presented quite a picture, as he stood on the judge's stand, which looked like an outhouse propped up on four poles. When you saw him there, all decked out in a blue suit, bow-tie, and a heavy felt hat, you knew right off who was in charge. Speaking into a large megaphone, he would announce the upcoming racing events with great authority. After giving the names of the horses and drivers in each race, he would then bellow: "Gentlemen, I want you to score your horses once by the grandstand, so that the audience can get acquainted with both horses and drivers in this big event. I then want the driver of the pole horse to bring the field up by the stand, and proceed up the track to the red flag, where he will turn his horse, with the other drivers following suit. Providing every horse is in its designated position, and none in front of the pole horse when you reach me, here at the judge's stand, I will yell "GO!" Make sure *no* horse is in front of the pole horse as you pass the stand!"

Well, Hilt's orders seemed to be simple enough. But, for some reason or other, the drivers always appeared to ignore them, so there were always three or four re-starts. Sometimes it took a half-hour to get the race underway.

Now, another thing that Hilt watched pretty closely was the posture of a driver sitting in a sulky. If all that was holding him on the cart was the fact that he had a tight grip on the reins, the judge would become a little suspicious. After taking a harder look, by peering over his glasses, he would sometimes make what he called, "An important judicial decision." "Gentlemen," he would shout over the megaphone, "it has been brought to my attention that the driver of such-and-such a horse is in no shape to perform his duties. I want the said driver removed, or the horse will be scratched." After a bit of argument with the driver, Hilt always managed to get his way. The suspect driver would be replaced, and the race would finally get underway.

It was thus that the little fairground tracks became the minor league of horse-racing, where many drivers learned their basic skills and went on to bigger and better things. The Kingston district alone produced some of the most colourful drivers ever to sit in a sulky: guys like Berny McKane, Guy LaRush, the Murphys, Joe and John, Charlie Gallagher, and Bernie Hunt. Around the Elgin-Westport area, there were Barney Davie, Earl Lake, and Norm Jones, who is still considered one of the better drivers on the big-time circuit.

Smiths Falls and the Ottawa Valley, however, topped everyone in producing great drivers: Bernard Grant; Wally King, Ken Carmichael; Chesterville's Caldwell brothers, Pem and Russ; Arnprior's Doc Findlay; the three Currans, Ross, Neil, and Rick; and the immortal Sted Craig. All of them were to eventually perform on tracks throughout Canada and the States.

I first met Sted, when I was a child of six, at the old Kingston fairgrounds. He had been a friend of my father's, and on that day, Dad and I stood at the side of the track to watch what was billed as the premier racing event of Eastern Ontario. It was a match race between the great Toll Gate, and the famous mare, Bertha Patch. Sted was the driver of Toll Gate, and Berny McKane was behind Bertha. As Sted was warming up his horse, he stopped and yelled to my Dad, "Tell Mickey to bet his money on old Toll." Well, Dad gave me a buck, and an old fellow standing beside us, Art Flannigan, covered the bet.

True to his word, Sted steered Toll Gate home, in what was then record time, nosing out the other horse, and I proudly pocketed the money. From then on I was a racing fan.

Well, it was nearly twenty years later when, like Sted, I had become a railroader, that I was introduced to the greatest and most colourful driver ever to come out of the Valley. I had gone over to see Sted work out his horses early one morning at the old Ryan's park in the Falls. He and Wally King were standing by the stable doors, and a young fellow, who looked to be in his teens, was out on the track, training a three-year-old colt.

Sted informed me that he had a sick horse and was waiting for the vet, a fellow we will call Doc F. You see, old Doc did not like too much publicity when he ws alive, so I presume I should honour his anonymity now that he is dead.

When Doc arrived, he took a gallon jug out of his car, came over to the stable, and asked Sted to show him which horse was ailing. Soon, he was pouring the liquid from the jug down the horses throat. After he'd poured off a third of the jug, he upped the bottle to his own lips, and lowered it another couple of inches. With that, he handed the bottle to Sted, who by this time was holding a tin cup in his hands. He filled the cup, poured it down, handed the cup and jug to Wally, and then it was my turn.

After everybody had done the honours, Doc put the jug in the window of the stable, with the sun beaming through, and he and Sted began to visit. Suddenly there was one hell of a bang, with glass flying everywhere. The jug had taken off like a rocket. Sted turned to Doc and said, "Ain't that stuff in the jug the same as you gave the horse?" "Yes, replied Doc," maybe you should let the horse out of the barn, now that he's feeling better." "What the hell says Sted," You mean I should get the horse out before she blows up too, and takes the barn with her?" "That's the general idea," old Doc replied, smiling.

Well, when they let the horse out to run, she did seem quite peppy, and while the three of us stood watching, the young lad who was training the colt came along. Sted introduced him as Ross Curran, and went on to say, "This young fellow is going to be one of the best drivers ever to sit in a sulky." And within five years, Sted's prediction came to pass.

Under Sted's tutelage, Curran quickly started making a name for himself at the various country fairs, and was soon overshadowing veterans with years of experience behind them.

Sted had recognized early that the kid had everything: good hands; cool in any situation; and, above all, fearless. While still in his teens, Curran was winning big at Connaught, driving against the best. Soon, he was the leading driver at Ottawa's Rideau Carleton and Montreal's Blue Bonnets.

Then, in the middle-sixties, he finally made it to the major league of racing: the Horse-Shoe Circuit – Greenwood, Mohawk, and St. Catharines. Within a year, after arriving on the Toronto circuit, he became the toast of the racing fans. At every race he appeared in hundreds of them would start shouting "Cowboy!" "Cowboy!" over and over again.

This nickname had been given to him early in his career, by his friend and fellow-driver, Pem Caldwell, when the two had been racing at Blue Bonnets. Pem watched with growing admiration as the young man won, in spite of driving really bad actors: horses that other drivers would have nothing to do with.

The story is still being told around the Greenwood race-track, in Toronto, that he was given his monicker the night he jumped from the sulky onto the horse's back. That was truly a night to remember! It seems he was coming down the home-stretch, with all the horses bunched together, when one of his lines broke. Realizing the risk to the other drivers, the Cowboy sprang from the sulky onto to the horse, and coolly guided it out of danger.

He did indeed drive some tough horses. For example, there was a speedy little fellow called Scootch. He was a lovable pet while home, with Ross's children all around him, and even beneath his feet. But when he got to the track his disposition changed entirely. He became completely ferocious, kicking and biting everything in sight. The only one who could get near him was the Cowboy himself.

Another bad one, although a great money-winner, was H.T. Navy, who not only hated people but other horses as well. When he was shipped to the track they had to make sure there were no horses in the stalls on either side of him. Ross's little daughter, Patty, remembered one time in Montreal when a lady-groom kept passing in front of Navy with a copper kettle in her hands. Ross warned her several times not to walk too close, but to no avail. Suddenly, Navy popped his head out and snatched the kettle. Then there was J.J. Tequilla, he, too, hated people and other horses. But most of all, he hated the sound of a bell. The phone in Ross's stable was right beside J.J.'s stall. He would only allow it to ring once before he would reach over and take it off the hook.

Regardless of how they behaved, however, Ross had a great affection for all the horses he drove. But of the three closest to his heart, one was Symbol Allen, a great old campaigner, owned by a Smiths Falls native, Less Ireland. Then there was Valour Dean. It was behind him, that Ross, at the age of sixteen, was to win his first major race, back in 1955. The other horse he spoke of fondly was Gayllon's Boy, who had a gold mane, and who always ran all out, as if every race might be his last.

For over ten years, from the middle-sixties till the late seventies, the Cowboy was a dominant figure, always in the top racing ten of North America. Known for his honesty and all-out efforts, he was a favourite with racing fans everywhere, whether in the country fair circuit, or the major tracks of both Canada and the United States.

During my own years of seclusion in Toronto, when I had quit going to the races, I gradually lost track of the Cowboy. The last time we had met had been back in the middle-seventies. It had been at the Orchard Park hotel, across from Greenwood race-track in Toronto. He was his usual jovial self, telling me racing tales, and filling me in on all the gossip around the Valley. Then, kiddingly, he mentioned that for the last little while he had been having trouble getting to sleep at night.

It seemed somebody had presented him with a monkey, and he called this new addition to the family, Buster. Somehow, Buster had developed a fondness for booze. Ross wouldn't have minded that so much, except for the fact that the monkey kept waking him up every two hours at night, demanding a shot. That did disturb him a bit.

Well, it was not until last Easter, when visiting Smiths Falls that I was sitting in my familiar haunt, the Lee Hotel, with some old-time Valley athletes: Joe Muldoon, John Halpin, and Ron Irwin. I began to inquire about the Cowboy. To my surprise, Irwin pointed to the fellow waiting on our table. He then introduced him as Ross's son, Doug, who was quite an athlete himself, having just finished the winter season playing hockey with the Perth Blue Wings.

He told me his father was not feeling too well, and was now in a nursing home, but his mother would be home at six that evening. He suggested I go over and have a visit.

Later, as I sat with the Cowboy's wife, Geraldine, and his young daughter Patty, I could feel the love and the pride they both had in the great horseman. Soon, there were pictures and write-ups littering the table in front of us, along with telegrams of congratulations the Cowboy had received over the years. There was a picture of Ross when he was a boy of five, riding on a cow. It seems that they had pastured the cow a mile away from the house, and it was Ross's job, at that tender age, to take the animal back and forth, for milking. So, instead of walking all that distance, he turned the cow into his first horse. There was another picture of his first win on Valour Dean, when he was only a kid of sixteen. We went on talking for over two hours.

Patty remembered the good days with her Dad on the race tracks across the country. Her favourite spots were the fall fairs in Upper New York State. Her eyes still sparkled when she spoke of her greatest thrill – at the big annual fair at Malone, N.Y. Here she was to meet the idol of her life, the country and western singer, Loretta Lynn. Her Dad had been the hero of the day, winning three races, and that night Loretta was billed as the main attraction for the evening entertainment. Ross, taking his daughter by the hand, introduced her to the singer, and Patty was speechless.

Like all kids, Patty loved fairs, especially in the States, where they allowed betting on the races. Ross would give ten dollars to each member of the family that had come along. He would tell them to bet on a certain race he would be driving in – it was always a sure thing, and the kids would, at the very least, triple their money. With thirty dollars in your pocket you could, at that time, take in all the rides and shows; gorge yourself on hot dogs, french fries, and soft drinks; and then have money left for souvenirs.

You knew right away that Patty, who was still in school, was also Daddy's girl. Like her father, she loved animals, having been around horses before she could walk. Her first pony was a little Albanian colt. It seems that a circus truck was passing through the district, when it met with an accident and rolled over, with six circus-trained ponies aboard. Ross, always the good Samaritan, kept the animals for months, until the owner finally had enough money to come and pick them up. All the Cowboy received, in the way of payment for room-and-board, was a little colt that had been born to one of the tiny mares while they had been staying with the Currans.

An older sister, Ann, who is twenty-three, is almost a veteran horsewoman herself, working as a groom for several years. Ann looked after the great trotter, Bobbo, for Norm Jones, the Morton race driver. Bobbo, was to win many prestigious races until his career came to an end last year.

Chuck, the oldest of the family, who was also away at the time of my visit, could well be another Cowboy. At the present time, he is working to obtain his driver's licence and, like his father, who trained under the best, he, too, has quite a mentor. This is none other than the famous Buddy Gilmore. Buddy, a world-class driver for years, and a Canadian to boot, is currently stabled at the big Meadowlands track in New Jersey.

I did not get to see Ross on my last visit, but I hear he is feeling better. Who knows? Maybe, sometime, we will see him back at the track, even if it's only for a little visit. Hopefully, Chuck will take up where his father left off.

Then, too, there is Patty. I watched as she sat, displaying the same ease her father had had in a sulky. I am certain that she, like her dad, will achieve the top, regardless of what profession she chooses in life.

In the meantime, you've got to get well again, Cowboy. The racing game and the world need colourful characters like you. Maybe I am asking for a miracle, but how great it would be if you could make one last curtain call. I can hear the fans now, standing in tribute, and shouting that old refrain: "Cowboy!" "Cowboy!" "Cowboy!"

My kind of people

9

Dollar Bill

It's time now to introduce you to some of my other friends, so let's move on to the city of Kingston, where I always drop in to the old Prince George Hotel, looking for company.

Well, this particular day was no different. I entered the Dollar Bill Lounge, and as my eyes slowly adjusted to the absolute darkness I head a voice say, "Hello Mike."

Who should be sitting at the head table, all alone, but my long-lost friend "Teenie" Harold Davis.

Now Teenie had boxed some good ones in his day in the Thirties, and had even gone the distance with famed Canadian lightweight, Sammy Luftspring, in a Kingston match-up.

Harold, like the other Kingston fighters of that era, fought most of his fights out of the old Kingston Locomotive Athletic Club on Ontario Street, just down aways from where we were sitting.

If anyone from Kingston could fill you in on the night life of Kingstonians during the Dirty Thirties it was Harold, as he had belonged to a gang of youths known as the "Forty Thieves."

Well, we got to talking about the sporting life in the Limestone

City during those Depression years, when we were joined by two arty-type strangers, who asked if they might share our table. One of the young men, called Walt, was so thin that he was almost at the point of emaciation. His body was as spare and tense as an unbaited mousetrap. He was carrying a large canvas, which all of his breed seem to carry, and he dropped it at his feet as he sat down.

After downing a double scotch, he began shuffling his feet as if he were keeping time to the vibrations in his head, as there was no music.

The other fellow was just the opposite in stature: short, with a bran-sack stomach. He had a fat, pock-marked face, framed with dirty, brindle hair which hung to his ass. His eyes had a glazed-cherry look, as if he were burning up with fever. He introduced himself as Lincoln, saying that he was a writer, and placed a sheaf of papers on the table.

Well, I looked over at Harold, and right off I knew that he was ready to leave, when all at once the silence was broken by Lincoln asking out of the blue, "Who in hell was Dollar Bill?" For a moment a smile hung on Harold's battle-scarred face and he replied in a rhyme:

> *Down by the river lived Dollar Bill*
> *He never worked and he never will.*

It was a rhyme that all Kingston children of the Thirties called out, when old Dollar Bill peddled by on his bike.

"Then there really was such a man?" Lincoln asked, ordering a round for the table. "Indeed there was," replied Harold, "but as a writer you should know that! One would think a man of your stature would have heard of that great play written by Robertson Davies, called *Fortune My Foe*." "Well, I did read that play," replied our friend of letters, "but I didn't know it referred to the same bootlegger whose name adorns these walls."

"I don't think Davies knew Dollar Bill all that well, but maybe he did." Harold replied. "Bill had many prominent friends and *he* could well have been one of them. Dollar was very discriminating, you know, when it came to people – except for children, who he loved dearly."

This said, Harold began to relate the story of Dollar Bill. To begin with, he stated that nobody seemed to know exactly where Bill had come from. Some said he was an American, and others said he had come from Western Canada. All agreed on one thing, however, that somewhere, sometime, Bill had run afoul of the law, and wherever he had come from, he had no intentions of going back.

The Dollar was a broad-shouldered, tough-looking character, but always clean and well-shaven. He had a grizzled face and unruly grey hair which seldom saw a comb. Pushed back on his head, he usually wore a fur cap with flaps that dangled about his enormous ears. It was only on the warmest days of the summer that he removed that old cap – and became years younger. Now it was rumoured about that Bill suffered all his life from bad head colds, and it was for that reason he always wore the cap. This could well have been true, for almost daily he would stop at his doctor's office across from the Hotel Dieu Hospital.

His physician was a doctor named "Shakey" Jakey, and Dollar was seen going in and out of his office on many a morning. Some say it was questionable as to who was doctoring whom, since there were often times when the good doctor needed a little medication himself.

Jakey was a character who could well have been a friend of Damon Runyon, although in appearance he looked more like an eccentric from Charles Dickens. He was a tiny dwarf of a man, with a hunchback, and he wore steel-rimmed glasses that hung over his nose. You were never quite sure, because of Doc's build, whether he was walking or crawling. Bill swore by him as a medical man – along with many other citizens of the time.

But getting back to Bill, he would remove his cap and dress fashionably to attend sporting events throughout the city – such as boxing at the Locomotive Gym, baseball at the Cricket Field, or Queen's football games at the old Richardson Stadium.

He would come to these events in style – in a big shiny Pierce Arrow – owned by one of his few close friends, Jack Sutherland. Jack was a millionaire who had taken to Bill the first time they met. It was Sutherland who paid all of Bill's fines when the police would deem it necessary to raid his establishment. The car was always chauffeured by a tiny Indian named Bill Dickson.

It was at one of the football games at the Stadium that Bill was to meet another one of his favourite people, Alfy Pierce.

Alfy, like Bill, had come to Kingston from nowhere, and had made his home at the Richardson Stadium, where he cleaned the dressing rooms. For years, he acted as mascot for the sports teams of that great institution of learning. Alfy was a tall, raw-boned black man, who always carried a cane and spoke in a rasping whisper.

Like many of Bill's friends, he enjoyed the odd drink. When his finances were such that he couldn't afford a little refreshment, he would sell his body to the university for medical research. When things would get financially better, he'd buy it back.

Well, there were times when he needed a drink, but his body belonged in whole to the university, so he had to turn to Bill, who helped him over many a rough spot. It was never recorded who owned Alfy's body when he died – the university or Bill. In all likelihood it was the university, as the Dollar passed away several years ahead of his friend.

Bill followed a definite daily routine. He did all his shopping in Kingston, and would cross the causeway on his bicycle with his ear-flappers flapping in the westerly breeze coming off Lake Ontario. Attached to the back of the bike was a rather large wooden box that served as a cache for his supplies, which he would bring back on his return.

His Kingston office was located at the Morrison Restaurant beside the *Whig-Standard*, and it was here that he made his social contacts and enjoyed some relaxed conversation each day. He would sit for hours, visiting, with a big black cigar dangling from his lips.

Next, he would go to the "Bull Dog" Milne bicycle shop, just down the street, where he'd have Milne check his bike to see that it was in order. From there it was on up Princess Street to the old Capital Theatre to park his bike, before he crossed the street to the Pappas pool room.

George Pappas was Bill's banker and financial advisor. In the corner of the pool room, behind the counter, stood a big black safe. Dollar would take George aside, and after a short conversation he'd deposit the previous night's take. The deposit would be mostly cash, but there was the odd cheque made out to Dollar Bill – a name which, I assure you, was as good as gold at the time. Bill's own signature, which has been preserved, was always the same: "$ Bill."

About once a month, Pappas would inform Dollar that his account was getting a little too big. It was then that the old bootlegger would make a few hundred-dollar withdrawals, and head out towards Portsmouth village.

Near the end of King Street stood St. Mary's Orphanage. Along the way, Bill would stop at the various stores and pick up clothing, candy, and toys, then head for the back door of the orphanage.

When he knocked, the same elderly Sister always came to the door. Without saying a word, he would hand her the little presents, along with an envelope which always contained at least a hundred dollars.

Leaving the orphanage as quietly as he had come, he would head back towards Kingston, where he'd have a secret meeting with another friend, Colly Gallagher. Colly had his own power boat, christened "Black Jack," which was faster than any boat on either side of the border. He was known locally during Prohibition as a rum-runner. He was also the only person at the time who could navigate the old channel which separated the two borders.

Now what went on during these conversations with Gallagher, we will never know; but – come to think of it – I guess there might be some connection between rum-running and bootlegging.

Another call Bill always made was to George Mahood's Ice Cream Parlour. Between George and Bill, the children of those tough times were kept happy with free cones.

As evening approached, he would peddle his way back across the causeway to prepare for a night of professional activity.

Now Bill's home and business establishment was a battered old sea-plane hangar, situated just west of the village of Barriefield, beside the Cataraqui River. Inside, that area reserved for customers was partitioned off into cosy little nooks by various improvised draperies. The furnishings weren't exactly luxurious, consisting mainly of somewhat beat-up chesterfields and armchairs, but they were comfortable enough.

Bill was as discreet in his business dealings as he was in his choice of friends. If you should drop into his place for a little refreshment, you paid fifty cents a glass for whatever soft drink you chose. Anything added to it came free, so he could never be accused of peddling alcoholic beverages. He also did not allow rowdies, minors, or women inside his place of business. If one were lucky enough to have a car in those days, the lady was required to remain seated in it. If she wished refreshment, she had to wait until her gentleman companion fetched some for her.

Ever since Bill had fallen afoul of the law, he regarded himself as an anti-authoritarian crusader. His mission in life was to circumvent the tyrannical government which forbade men the right to have a drink at will.

He knew that it was impossible to have the Prohibition Law repealed, so he did the next best thing, and ignored it. He supplied refreshments for those who felt inclined to partake. "If you're not a part of the solution you're a part of the problem," he would proudly say.

Bill kept no booze in his shack, as the law at the time forbade alcoholic beverages be kept by an unauthorized person for sale on land. Because of this, Bill kept his liquor hidden in the cool waters of the Cataraqui River, just behind his shack.

He prided himself on the respectability of his premises. He closed down at midnight, and only very special friends were granted after-hour privileges. These included, it was said, the magistrate, crown attorney, and the police chief of the day.

Should a rowdy or a stranger disturb his peace after the closing hour, he would frighten the intruder away with a blast from his shotgun, which he always kept near the door.

Oh, he had his trying days like everybody else – especially when there was a police raid. To make things appear on the up-and-up, he would be levied a heavy fine – but he never spent an hour in jail. The fines would be paid by one of his influential friends, such as Gallagher, and the judicial system of the day saw to it that he remained free to go about his important business.

To the end, Bill, a complex soul, thought he was doing right; and although he lived like a pauper, he gave thousands away to charity.

The end finally came one fall day, just after the war. Bill left as quietly as he had come. It was days later – November 4, 1945 – when a friend found him lying at rest on the cabin floor. "Do you mean to say that nobody missed old Bill when he passed away?" asked Walt – the only words that had been spoken since Harold began his tale.

"Oh yes," he replied "he was indeed missed by his real friends, the children, but it was many months before they knew. They thought he had only gone away on a visit. Who would tell a child, especially an orphan, that Santa Claus was dead?"

Well, the fire had disappeared from the artist's eyes, drowned out by tears, and Harold stood up to leave.

"What was Bill's real name?" the artist asked.

"That my friend is a secret, know only to a chosen few," said Harold as he walked slowly towards the door, with me close on his heels.

When we had reached the street, he took my hand, and gripping it tightly said:

"I hope it's not twenty-five years before we meet again." Then bending down, still clutching my hand he whispered in my ear "Bill's name, my friend, was William J. M....., but he was always known locally as Bill Allen. He spent many a year like those little orphans, behind a stone wall. Maybe sometime when you're in Portsmouth Village you'll look over at that old prison wall and think kindly of Bill, as I always do. But most of all I hope you remember his words: 'If you're not a part of the solution you're a part of the problem.'"

My kind of people

10

Eddy "Squire" Bennett – and the Beings from Outer Space

Years ago, in the village of Westport there lived a tiny elf of a man with a weatherbeaten face, which he kept half hidden by a large black hat pulled down over his brownish nose. Squire Bennett, being a man of no visible means of support, somehow managed to get through life without toil. He ate well and drank even better.

Now there were some in the community with faulty educations and little respect, who called him another name because of his dark complexion. I assure you that such a name would not be tolerated today. Why, just the other day I was reading where an old school chum of mine, Tom Sullivan, the present mayor of Arnprior, used just such a name regarding something being lost in the woodpile and the Human Rights Commission is raising hell. If the Squire were alive today he would tell those fellows in Ottawa that we need more humans and less commissions.

Eddy (you could call Mr. Bennett "Eddy" if you were one of his chosen people), had squatter's rights on the Canadian National Railway property, where the old Westport station stands. It was a choice enough lot, but his home was somewhat less elaborate, as it was just a tiny shack, abandoned by the railway.

The Squire often said that someday he would gather his friends together, under the direction of his closest buddy, Morgan Mullville, to build a mansion. Due to his many social commitments however, he never got around to it.

Mr. Bennett was very discriminating when it came to choosing his friends, confining them to such professionals of the community as Doctors Hamilton and Goodfellow, and a few storekeepers like Barney Davey. There were a few other people he tolerated on a social basis only, like "Slow" Joe McCann and me.

If you were a social friend he would grant you an audience, providing you presented the proper credentials and the correct password. The credentials consisted of two bottles of wine, and the password was, "It's the Old Sailor." Old Sailor was the Squire's favourite brand of tonic. So if you happened to have *more* than the minimum entrance fee of two bottles, the Squire would greet you with a hearty "Hello, ain't I glad to see you!"

It was not until one October evening when Joe and I arrived with a full case that the Squire accorded us a truly regal reception and invited us for a feast.

Eddy was known far and wide for his chicken stew. The Squire claimed it was the freshness of his chicken that made the stew so delicious. I might add that several farmers in the district complained about losing the odd chicken, and it was even hinted around that some of those birds might have found their way into Eddy's pot. Yet, there was never a feather to be seen at his residence.

I do know, however, that after numerous complaints, a provincial policeman, Cliff Perry, began a little investigation. He watched the Squire as he took his leisurely morning stroll, carrying his shopping basket. On one occasion, as he was walking past Herman Pine's market garden, the officer stopped the Squire and inquired as to what he had in the basket. The Squire replied that he had a few vegetables which Mr. Pine, in his generosity, had given him. The officer took a look, however, and spied two chickens. Well, if Cliff was surprised, he didn't show it half as much as Eddy. "By Gad," sayeth the Squire, "Pine must have given me the wrong basket!"

But getting back to the night that Joe and I were given the royal treatment – after the feast, and a long visit, where the three of us had solved most of the world's problems – the Squire looked out the door and spied a full moon. Checking to see that we still had a good supply of the Old Sailor, he informed us that he would like to visit his dear friend, "Spaceman" Sodden, who lived on the mountain.

As we drove along the mountain road, Squire explained to Joe that Sodden was an astronomer of sorts, who performed most of his scientific work when the moon was in full bloom. He then went on to say that the Spaceman knew a great deal regarding the science of the unknown. He hinted that Joe and I might even be the first of our generation to witness some little-known secrets concerning Outer Space.

When we pulled up to the Sodden house, there was neither movement nor lights, only the moon smiling down. The Squire told Joe and me to remain in the car, as his astronomer friend would not want to be disturbed, especially on nights when there was a full moon. Before leaving the car he took two bottles of Old Sailor, promising that he would be back in no time. Well, it wasn't no time, but he did make it back an hour or so later, informing us that the great one would see us.

Standing beside the outhouse, and peering into the sky through two empty wine bottles, stood our new-found friend of letters. Motioning for us all to be quiet, he began a blow-by-blow description of what was about to unfold. "Those two ships almost collided," he yelled and then putting down his wine-bottle binoculars, he invited us into his darkened home.

Fetching four pint jars (a little sticky, with honey still clinging to their sides), he explained that social drinkers should never been seen drinking from a bottle.

After downing a couple of jars, and wiping his lips with the bib of his overalls, he began his lecture on Outer Space. He explained that he had discovered his mountain farm was the centre of the universe: everything that crossed the sky, whether it be space ships, planes, or migrating geese, must pass directly above his outhouse, where he took all his sightings. His two-holer, he said, was some .00001 degrees south of where we were now sitting. Years ago, when there was only about one plane a month, he had begun his study of Outer Space. It was not until the beginning of the war, when planes became more numerous, that he noticed everything travelling through the sky, whether it was going north, east, south, or west, must pass his lookout. Then he told us in a rather hushed voice that there were spaceships from other planets, not only passing overhead, but landing in his pasture.

After we had finished a couple more jars, Professor Sodden began his preparation for our field trip. He constructed a pair of field glasses out of empty wine bottles for each of us, and we made our way to the look-out. As we peered up into the sky, the Squire got a sighting. "There's a ball of fire coming our way now!" he yelled suddenly.

Sodden trained his glasses in the same direction and coolly announced, "That's the one from Mars."

With that, the four of us, falling over each other, escaped to the safety of the old farm house, locking the door behind us. After a little more refreshment, the Prof explained calmly that there was no need to be afraid. He went on to say that the occupants of that particular saucer were no bigger than horseflies, although they could converse in English. He added that the only reason he had hurried us into the house was because his friends might not tolerate strangers.

After a few minutes, he started a fire in his old wood stove, explaining as he worked that the smoke billowing out of the chimney was a pre-arranged signal that all was well. To be frank, I don't know how much smoke got up the chimney, but there sure as hell was enough of it billowing into the house. Then Sodden left to greet his friends.

He had hardly gotten through the door when there was a deep, humming noise, followed by the invasion of thousands of little objects, apparently coming from nowhere.

Well, the rest of us all seemed to lose interest in Outer Space at the same moment. The Squire was the first out the door, followed closely by me and Joe. The last thing I heard was the scientist, somewhere in the dark night, saying, "Good-bye." Yet to this day I'm not quite sure whether he was talking to us or his friends from Mars.

Well, as you can imagine, that experience bothered the Squire and me for quite some time. But Joe brushed it off as just another adventure. "Slow" was never the worrying type. However, we finally decided to go see another one of our friends who was wise in the ways of the community, and what was going on.

He was Patty Smith, the local road commissioner. Because of his job, he had visited every farm in the area at one time or another. He also knew a little choice gossip about everybody. When the Squire told Patty what was bothering us, Patty nodded knowingly, and stated that, indeed, there had been some strange things going on around the Sodden farm. He hastened to say, however, that he blamed these occurrences on earthmen rather than the inhabitants of other planets.

Then pondering a bit, like all great men of wisdom, he told the Squire there was one thing for certain he *did* know. Sodden always kept bees in his chimney, and every fall he smoked them out and retrieved the honey. When the Squire told Patty that what we had seen that night was bigger than bumble bees, our philosopher friend was lost for an answer.

"Come to think of it," he said, 'you don't see many bumble bees on a cold October night."

There's never a full moon that I don't look up in the sky and think of Squire, Spaceman, and Joe. One of these days I'll be hearing from one of them, and we'll all meet up at the look-out.

So long, friends, till we meet again.

My kind of people

11

"Mr x"–the Falcon of the Valley

I had left the Ottawa Valley a few months before Harry Falconer McLean died. I never knew his middle name until I read his obituary in a Toronto paper that sad spring day in 1961. Somehow I wish now that I had known, for there is no name that could have better described him.

Like a falcon, his steel grey head towering over everybody, he'd swoop into one of the various Valley hotels. His piercing eyes would soften when he'd give out with a grin and the thundering invitation "Let's have a party!" Oh what a party! They'd last for days.

When he wasn't partying he loved to fly. One of his flying escapades took him and his nurse, Ruth Atkinson, around the world in 1939. When someone asked him on his return the reason for such a journey, his answer was, "For my health."

I first met Harry in the late forties, when I was a cub reporter in Smiths Falls. He was always a little distant with newspapermen – never wanting to be interviewed. "Railroad men don't *talk* about things," he'd tell you, "They *do* them." So, it wasn't until I became a railroader that I ever learned anything about the man himself.

I remember one frosty January night we were sitting in the Rideau Hotel in Smiths Falls, watching the patrons come in shivering from the sub-zero cold. As an old railroader, Bill Powell, was dusting the frost from his brow, Harry looked over and said, "Twenty below is nothing. You should spend a winter in North Dakota."

He went on to tell us that he had been born to Canadian parents in Bismarck, North Dakota. His father, John, originally from Prince Edward Island, had been the town's first mayor. His mother, of whom he spoke fondly, was Mary Falconer from Glengarry County. The county of his youth is on every North Dakota map. *McLean County*, he would proudly say.

Born to the frontier and reared on its romance, his childhood was spent listening to stories of Wild Bill Hickock and his death in Deadwood; of highwaymen who lay in wait for the Deadwood stage; of marching soldiers and Sioux Indians. The West was just being settled, as covered wagons still passed through on their way to Wyoming and Montana. There was the occasional bad man, and countless reminders of Indian warfare.

His father was a storekeeper at Fort Lincoln, as well as a teamster on the stage-coaches which ran through the barren badlands between Bismarck and its new gold camp of Deadwood. His mother waltzed with Custer at the Regimental Dance on a June night in 1876. She heard the call of the boots and saddles in the early morning. She saw the young general ride away with the fighting Seventy toward Little Big Horn, never to return.

Harry told of riding to school on horseback and delivering papers on the same horse, in order to make enough to send himself to the North Dakota Business College. After graduating, he journeyed to Minneapolis, where he became a water-boy with the Weston Railroad and Construction Company. Step by step he went up the ladder of progress: from time-keeper; to Construction Superintendent; to General Manager; and, finally, to being part-owner of his own company and several conglomerates.

As a water-boy, he saw men maimed for life and carried away to receive insufficient first aid. Sometimes the result of an injury would be deformity – but often it was death. After the job had been completed, no one seemed to remember those who had been hurt or killed, or the hundreds of labourers who slaved in the blazing sun and cold Arctic blizzards. As a result – once Harry reached a position of influence – he was forever after concerned with the workingman's welfare.

His first company was formed in 1905, when he and his friend, Jim Therrien, became partners. Their initial contract brought them across the border to Canada. At last, he was established in the country he loved – as he'd always proclaimed himself a Canadian.

It was tough going the first few years, and they had to take in a new partner, Homer Black. Thus, the company became known as the Homer Black Co. Ltd., probably because he had the most money. In its thirty-odd years of existence, the three partners formed connections with four big construction outfits, the chief of which was the Dominion Construction Company. Harry became president of Dominion in 1913. This conglomerate built enough railways and branch lines to stretch all the way across Canada. Yet, somehow, history has neglected Harry. With all of his accomplishments, and his works of genius in construction, he has never received his rightful recognition.

To fully record his achievements would require years of research, as his private papers and memoirs have disappeared. Down through the years, I began many stories about Harry, but was never able to complete any of them. I did, however, read all the reports I could find, and saved numerous clippings. Yet even the clippings seem today to be inaccurate – with many dates questionable. To give just one example, the recording of his death in the Toronto papers, stated that he had died on April 30, 1961. In truth he died on April 23rd, and was buried in Notre Dame cemetery, off Côte de Neiges, in Montreal.

Among the many memories of his ventures which I particularly savoured were the pushing of a tunnel a hundred miles from the Catskill watershed to New York City; and the building of the Lincoln and Holland Tunnels, in the Thirties.

During the First World War, he was made an honorary Colonel for life, when he formed a regiment out of the railway engineers. They were the best in the world. They restored the bombed-out railways of France, making it possible for the allies to transport badly needed troops and tanks.

In the Second World War, he joined forces with the Canadian

Government to build airports and vital industrial plants – such as the ammunition factory in Valleyfield, Quebec.

An American magazine of the period reported that his firm fulfilled a staggering hundreds of millions in contracts – which would make him worth even more in today's currency. But of all his accomplishments, there were two of which he seemed most proud: the building of the Flin Flon Railway, and the Abitibi Dam.

The Flin Flon job came about because of a tremendous find of copper ore, about a hundred miles north of the Pas, in northern Manitoba. The mine had been sold to the Whitney interests in New York, and McLean got the contract by convincing their engineers that he could save a year on the building of the road. The road was started, and it tentacled along the frozen muskeg, around hills and across windswept lakes. Finally a skeleton branch was laid. Truckloads of ballast covered the ice, and acted as insulation to prevent it from melting, as the frozen mush below remained solid. The job was finished a year ahead of time, and Harry received a $250,000 bonus.

True to the promise he made to himself as a water-boy, Harry didn't forget his workingmen. When the job was finished, he erected a plaque in their honour. It still stands today, where the Flin Flon railway juts from its main line. It reads: IN LOVING MEMORY OF THOSE WHO WORKED AND DIED HERE, and was one of several such plaques that he had erected through the years.

According to his long-time chauffeur, Harry Durant, the other project he liked to talk about in the privacy of his home was the Abitibi Power Dam, seventy miles north of Cochrane, and the tremendous difficulties involved in constructing it. Today, it supplies electric power to many isolated towns of the lonely north.

Durant said Harry would often call him into the office at his Merrickville home, just to talk about building the dam. "It got so that after a couple of years, I knew every detail of that project," Durant told me recently. Harry could be justly proud of that undertaking, and prouder of the way he used his men. Again, when the job was completed he erected another plaque:

IN LOVING MEMORY
OF THOSE WHO WORKED AND DIED HERE
THE SONS OF MARTHA

The last line, "The sons of Martha," was taken from a poem by Kipling, referring to the parable of Mary and Martha. The poem became his men's worksong, and every man, regardless of his nationality or difficulty with the language, could recite it. Thus, all of them became known as the "Sons of Martha."

After completion of the railroad in The Pas, Harry took on another job in the Maritimes. For some reason, he fell behind schedule and a large penalty was involved. The men from The Pas were quick to show their loyalty and love for him. Layed-off, and seven hundred strong, the men made their way to the Maritimes and bailed him out, paying their own fares, which amounted to $50,000! The job was finished on time.

It was the Valley people Harry loved the most, and on whom he showered his many unpublicized gifts of kindness. We'll never know how many mortgages he paid off in the community, or how many hungry families he fed. And his generosity extended far beyond the Valley. Stories are now legend about his charitable deeds in the various cities of Eastern Canada – from Halifax to Windsor.

In his later years, only two classes of people seemed to upset him – nosey newspapermen and overzealous policemen. I was with him twice when he encountered the police in Smiths Falls. The first incident occurred when he kicked out a plate glass window in the Rideau Hotel; and the second, when he managed to stop the Old Home Week parade by standing in the middle of Beckwith Street, and refusing to budge during the summer of '50. On both occasions he was wearing a derby hat and a coonskin coat – on what happened to be the two warmest days I ever recall in the Valley.

The well-known photographer, T.V. Little of Ottawa, and I, bailed him out on that second occasion. We went to the Russell Hotel, where we weren't as well known, so Harry could get his bearings. Sitting over a refreshing drink he told us a story about another encounter he had had with the police in 1944, in Windsor. While visiting that city on one of his escapades, somebody whispered in his ear that the police department was in need of money for its burial fund. "I always liked policemen," he told his informer. "In fact I like them so well that I'm willing to contribute generously to help bury them," he joked, laughing uproariously.

Then there was a time they locked him up in Halifax for a little disturbance. His chauffeur, Harry Durant, was with him on that occasion. This time, he paid his fine quietly, and after returning to Merrickville sent the jail a cheque for $5,000 with a note saying, "Clean up the joint!"

With all due respect to many historians, who seemed to think that Harry was a show-off, who just performed to gain notoriety, I must state that no one who knew him well believed this. I guess you'd have to have lived in the Valley to understand such a man, who the outside world saw as a showman in search of an audience. In truth he was a lonely, kindly man who loved people and loved to laugh. In return, he'd provide a few laughs himself, and give his money to those he believed in need. Several editorials of the day criticized the way in which he handled his money; but they only knew of the careless way in which he spent small sums, not of the thousands he gave quietly to the desperate. They headlined him as "Mr. x, the showman" rather than as the great Harry McLean, the hardworking construction contractor with a heart of gold. They never acknowledged him as the genius who built more railroad branch lines in our Dominion than any other person, before or since.

So, although I'll mention a few of Harry's well-publicized escapades, I'll not dwell on them. I want Harry to be remembered for what he was: a man who could lay a mile-and-a-half of railway track a day; a man who opened up Canada's vast northwest; and a man who should go down in history as a great Canadian – right up there with Van Horne.

It was long before I met him that he became known nationally as "Mr. x," during the Depression years of the Dirty Thirties, when he would visit Toronto's King Edward Hotel and drop ten and twenty-dollar bills from the windows. He loved to watch the joy in the streets below, as passersby ran to retrieve them. His private donations ranged from a $5,000 gift to a hospital, to a $2,000 cheque for a five-month-old boy, the son of a taxi driver. His biggest give-away was in the city of Windsor, where it is reputed he handed out $50,000 in cheques and large bills, and it was here that his bank manager stepped in to take over the reins.

The true identity of "Mr. x" was not revealed until November, 1943, in Halifax. All the reporters who had reported his exploits over the years knew who he was. But none of them had blown his cover until one day in Halifax. He had browbeaten and cajoled them all into a promise not to mention his real name, even if their editors requested stories about his strange philanthrophies. But that day in Halifax, the bubble burst, and many thought his generosity would come to an end. They just weren't smart enough to realize Harry's true reason for keeping his identity secret. Once it was known, an avalanche of letters began to arrive at his Merrickville home. Letters from as far away as Mexico! There were days when he would receive a hundred or more, and although some read like Hollywood fan mail, many others were pleas for money.

He described much of that mail as heartbreaking, and would reply with a donation to the letters that touched the most. Yet even a millionaire couldn't begin to satisfy all the requests. It was the thought of having to refuse so many of these unfortunate people that caused Harry to become despondent – and even more so during the last few years of his life. But he did continue to be a philanthropist; and when he made trips to Ottawa and Toronto, he was still followed by herds of reporters.

During the war, he often visited the wounded veterans in the Christie Street Hospital in Toronto. He would leave about three thousand dollars on each of his whirlwind tours of the various wards. On one such visit, accompanied by Dante the Magician, he walked into one large ward shouting, "Are we winning the war?" The reply was a deafening "Yes!"

A card at the head of one bed carried the name "Sgt. W.J. McLure." "Aha! Another good Scotsman," said Harry, sitting himself down for a ten minutes visit. As he left, he put two one hundred dollar bills on the bed, but not before telling McLure, "Some goofy reporter used my name in the paper when I gave away a little confetti in Halifax a week ago. Ever since then, all sort of people have written me – some of them, crazy women who want to marry me. I'm not interested in crackpots, but I do want to do something for you fellows." Dante the Magician looked around the room with tears in his eyes. He began to help big Harry distribute money to every man in the ward and every room on the floor. His last donation was ninety-five cents in American change to a lone soldier. It was all the money he had left in his pocket.

That night, as he watched Dante perform at a Toronto hotel, Harry felt sorry for the supporting cast of twelve girls who had accompanied the magician from New York. It was a rather chilly

October evening, and the girls weren't dressed for the Canadian cold. Harry went out and purchased a fur coat for each of them. The coats were so expensive that when the American girls tried to cross the border again they were unable to pay the duty.

Someone in Merrickville asked Harry if he had also been stuck with the duty charges. "No," he replied, "I told Dante to make the coats disappear, until the girls got across the border."

Gradually, Harry faded from the limelight, spending more and more time in his big stone mansion in Merrickville. But again, like the falcon, he'd occasionally swoop into one of the hotels of the Valley and buy for the house, slipping out to pull the fire-alarm and wake up the town. By now, however, the parties were shorter, never lasting for over a day.

The residents of Merrickville saw Harry daily through the fifties, after he withdrew from the outside world. Most people must have found him a little eccentric. When he strolled down the streets, he was usually dressed only in pajamas and a housecoat. And he was always prominent on Fair days, when he'd ride a donkey, or lead the Scottish pipe band.

He also continued to entertain politicians from Ottawa, who came looking for handouts and parties. One night when five prominent cabinet members of the time arrived, notifying Harry beforehand that they wanted to have a barbecue, he had things set up outside on the lawn. That day it had turned cold, so Harry hid all the blankets and warm clothing. When the guests arrived they were all invited outdoors, where Harry sat in his coonskin coat, while the others froze in their summer suits. It was one of the few occasions he didn't have to ask his guest to leave at a proper hour.

Near the last, Harry became embittered by many of his political friends, but always seemed to have a warm spot for Mackenzie King – although he didn't mind insulting him when he felt the occasion called for it.

His chauffeur, Durant, once described to me a particular visit to King's home. As they drove in, Harry saluted King's two RCMP guards with the words, "Why don't you fellows get lost." King, hearing him come to the door, said, "I see you're drunk again Harry; the same as yesterday when you sent me a truckload of roses. What do you propose I do with all those flowers?" "Send them to your girl friends in Hull," was Harry's reply, as the two entered King's residence.

C.D. Howe became a growing thorn in Harry's side, because the government had begun to get after him for back taxes. Harry would call Howe almost daily, to give him a piece of his mind. So gradually, many of Harry's affluent friends no longer came to visit him, since they did not want to be associated with his tax problems. As a result, he became increasingly lonely.

When village life became unbearable, he'd travel about the world, hunting in Africa or sightseeing in Paris – but he always returned to his beloved Merrickville. There he would wander about, stopping to play with children, and again pulling the fire-alarm when he thought things were a little too quiet. Sundays he found the quietest day of all, and on one occasion he casually walked down the main street, taking his cane to all the store windows along the route – even the large rounded bank window which, because of its design, took two weeks to replace.

At night, if he became restless, he'd drive the back roads in his old Packard. When the roads were closed by snow, he would use his specially designed snowmobile. He always chose the shortest distance between two points: a skill he had learned in the construction business. Whether it was fence, garden, or cedar hedge, he plowed his way through – paying for the damage later.

Up until the last few years, he kept his plane, with a private pilot, Dick Preston. Together they'd fly about the district. On one occasion he took off without Preston, and zoomed about the village shaking every window for miles. When he finally landed he was met by the Provincial Police, who levelled him with a two-hundred-dollar fine for flying without a licence. He had possessed a pilot's licence at one time, but since he could never find anyone with the courage to accompany him when he was at the controls, he had given it up.

So, during this latter period, when the outside world heard little about Harry, Merrickville citizens saw him constantly.

After reading his obituary in the Toronto paper, I started to rewrite my story about Harry, but again I was unable to finish. Then, quite recently, while I was visiting the town of Prescott, I ran into one of his old friends, Bob Moffat, who told me many enjoyable stories about him, but insisted that if I wanted to find out about the real Harry, I should go to Merrickville, and visit with some of the townspeople. "Forget about Harry's construction feats," Bob said, as I was leaving, "Write about the man and his kindness. He was the most generous man to ever set foot in the Valley. Tell of his weaknesses, too. Harry wouldn't mind, for all of them belong to every man. But most of all tell of his great love for children, the desolate, and the poor."

The little village looked the same, as I drove over the narrow bridge. When I approached the big stone mansion, I pulled to the side of the road. I looked in through the front window, to see the room filled with elderly residents. With all due respect, it still looked empty. For me, it *was* empty, because there was no Harry to make an appearance.

I drove on through the village to the Merrick Hotel, parked my car, and went inside. Two old-timers were sitting at the bar. I asked them if they remembered Harry McLean. They both smiled, and in unison replied, "Who could forget him?" "Can you tell me anything about him that I could use in a story?" I asked, buying them each a beer. Finally, the elder of the two said, "Weren't you a railroader around these parts at one time?" "Yes," I replied. So he advised me to look up another railroader, by the name of Glen Burchell, a couple of blocks from the hotel.

I located Glen in his modern village bungalow. He hadn't changed a great deal over the years, still as healthy-looking as in his younger years, when he was a well-known athlete around the Valley. "I've come to write a story about Harry McLean," I said, as he opened the door with a beaming smile. "My God! Harry McLean! I was just thinking about him the other day. He made my childhood; and he made this town!"

When we were both seated I asked him if he could tell me how he had seen Harry through the eyes of a child.

"To me, as a child," he began, "Harry was everything. He was a king living in a mansion – Santa Claus, every day of the year, handing out presents – and the world's greatest clown, who was funnier than the great Emmet Kelly." Growing up in the village with Harry, he said, was like living in the land of make-believe. Harry supplied apples and milk to the school, for the children to have at recess. "At Christmas, you told your teacher what you wanted for a present, and Harry saw that you got it on Christmas Day."

After school, the children would run to Harry's backyard to ride the little Shetland ponies he kept there. If some child happened to fall in love with a particular pony, Harry would make it a gift. As a result, he would give away dozens of ponies in the course of the year.

In the summertime, the children would swim at a beach Harry had laid out for them – including benches with big sun-shades. During the winter, they played on his toboggan slide, where he supplied toboggans, skis, and any other necessary equipment. He also built a rink and provided skates, hockey sticks, and even hockey gloves.

On Fair days, he would organize foot races for all the children. Even the contestants who finished last would receive five dollars. Harry's old friend, Stan Knapp, had a full-time job looking after the rinks, the slides, the beach, and ball fields.

On days when he wanted to make the kids laugh, he'd gather them all on Main Street, and tear up ten dollar bills, throwing the bits up in the air, and then watch them rush to retrieve the pieces. The big game after that was matching the torn bits which they could then take to the bank.

He would also let them play with the animals in his miniature zoo, but told them to stay away from his parrot. It seems the parrot's language contained a few choice swear words, that Harry felt might corrupt the children.

On winter days he used to take them for rides behind his team of huskies. Sometimes, he'd take a group to Smiths Falls or Brockville, to one of the furniture stores. Each child was asked to pick out a present for their mother – presents which ranged from radios to coal stoves.

Yes, a childhood influenced by Harry was something nobody could forget. But, as Glen went on to say, little was known about Harry's private life, his two marriages, or the goings-on in the big house. "You'd have to talk to his chauffeur about that." So the two of us made our way to Harry Durant's.

"Harry McLean?" Durant began, "He made my life! Some days, he fired me as often as five times. Then, a half-hour later, he'd be looking for me. During the hectic years of working with him, interrupted when I went overseas to the war, until I finally felt I must leave him, he often said, 'If there's anything in the world you want, just let me know.'"

"Would you tell me about the two wives?" I asked.

"Well, his first wife was Irene Robertson. Sometimes when he was in his cups he'd talk about her. He loved her dearly, but something came between them over the years."

She came from a wealthy family and, like Harry, she loved children. Durant told of seeing Irene whenever she visited Merrickville. Like Harry, she was often extremely lonely. It is believed they probably grew apart when Harry was away for long periods on construction jobs. The last time Durant saw Irene was when he drove her to her apartment in Toronto, where she died in 1942.

The other woman in Harry's life was Rita Fitzpatrick, from Montreal, who had come to the McLeans when she was only a child. She remained with Harry the rest of his life.

Durant spoke loyally of Rita – of the way she looked after Harry, and of the things she had to endure. She nursed him when he was sick, accompanied him on all of his trips, and sheltered him from the greedy. She ruled the household with an iron hand, which, at times, was certainly necessary. According to Durant, she was a *real* lady.

"Did Harry have any brothers or sisters?" I asked. "Yes," he replied, "he had one brother, Bill. A fine big fellow. He used to come to Merrickville to visit Harry. He wouldn't stay for any length of time, however, and would say to Harry, 'Two McLeans can't get drunk at the same time.' Then, when Bill would ask me to drive him to the train, Harry would take this as another occasion to fire me if I complied."

On the way to the station with Bill, Durant was informed that every month he was receiving a thousand dollars from Harry, and was always sending it back. Harry would immediately return the money, and Bill would eventually deposit it in the bank.

When I asked why Harry had settled in Merrickville in the first place, Durant said that he often told him he thought it was the most beautiful village in the world, and the old stone mansion appealed to him greatly. He also became associated there with a local man by the name of Dekes, with whom he formed a partnership in the Grenville Crushed Rock Co. It was the best crushed rock of its day, as can be testified today by the double track laid between Perth and Montreal. Perhaps there is no smoother track in the world. I can vouch for that myself, having travelled it often.

As I left, Durant came with me to the door, and his parting words were, "I still miss him. The village will never be the same."

But I still wanted to find out more about Harry's personal life – especially his relationship with his two wives. So, bidding Glen goodbye, I headed towards my cousin, Margaret Maloney's, village. She had nursed Harry years before.

Again, I was greeted with a warm smile at the mention of his name, and Margaret led me into her house. "He was a great man and a real gentleman – when he wasn't drinking – and many were the long walks I took with him. Almost daily, when he was about the house, we would walk back a mile to the pond where he fed the ducks and geese. He'd always have his pockets filled with corn, and along the way he'd stop and admire nature. He was like a child when he was drinking though; and if you crossed him and didn't say you were sorry, he wouldn't forget it. At times when he had too much to drink he would be almost violent, but he always said, 'I like Margo, she never gets me drunk.'"

I asked Margaret, as a woman, what *she* thought of the relationship between Harry and his two wives. She was quiet for a long time and finally replied, "I'm not quite sure. He loved them both, but in two different ways."

She went on to say that she was with Harry when Irene passed away in a Toronto apartment fire in the early forties; and helped him to sort through some of her personal belongings which were sent to Merrickville. She knew that he was deeply hurt and sadly attended Irene's funeral.

With Rita, it had been like a father-child relationship in the years before they were married. As a young woman, she had promised Harry that she would look after him all of his life, and she more than fulfilled that promise. Margaret told of nights when she and Rita would have to go and fetch Harry from his visits to friends, after he became obnoxious. There were also occasions, in the various hotels across the country, when it fell to Rita to get him away from people who tried to get him drunk to pry money from him. When I asked the rather leading question of why the two married, she thought again awhile, and then replied, "Harry had been Rita's whole life. She had given all her years to the man she loved. As for Harry, he came to realize that the woman who cared for him most all those years, asked nothing in return."

On my way back to Toronto, I had reached Kingston when I realized there was one more call I had to make, to an elderly priest who lived in Napanee. Father John O'Neil was with Harry right up until his passing.

I knew he was the only person left who could tell me about Harry's final days. "I suppose you were one of Harry's drinking friends?" the ageing priest said softly, when I introduced myself and told him why I had come.

"Harry was the greatest, loneliest, and most complex man I have ever met," he went on, "but I'm a better man for having known him so well."

He told me of coming to Merrickville in 1948, and remaining there until a few months after Harry's death in 1961. He said that Harry would send for him, or phone him, or come to the rectory himself. You never knew what the situation would be; but he was always a gentleman.

"He was more than courteous with all clergymen, regardless of creed, but there were times when I had to tone him down a bit. There were also times when he put on quite a show, but he never hurt anyone except himself.

"He had a terrific knowledge of religion, politics, and history; and he read extensively. He could talk on any subject of the day, and loved to quote poetry. His two favourite poems, when he'd been drinking a little, were Kipling's "Sons of Martha," and Cooper's "Last of the Mohicans."

He travelled extensively about the world and, like Hemingway, he loved to hunt. Yet with all his wealth and adventures, the only true solace he found was in his Merrickville home with his few close friends. Night after night, when he asked me to come up for a steak supper, we'd talk on every subject imaginable. I enjoyed the visits but not the steaks. They were never properly cooked. Your plate would be filled with blood."

When I asked Father O'Neil if he had officiated at Harry's second marriage (because there still seemed to be too many questions in that regard), he replied, "Harry and Rita were married in Salisbury, South Rhodesia. One day I was sitting in my office when a long-distance call came from a priest in Rhodesia. He asked me if I knew Harry McLean and Rita Fitzpatrick, and if they were free to marry. I told him that they were, so the ceremony took place. From Rhodesia, they travelled to Rome, where Harry had an audience with the Pope, whom he presented with a substantial gift."

This time, when Harry returned to Merrickville he seemed to be more settled. He still continued to drink, but confined most of his drinking to home and the company of friends.

He continued his battle with C.D. Howe and many members of the Cabinet, and kept on giving them hell. After the Ottawa politicians stopped coming to his home in Merrickville. Harry seemed glad in a way, although a little put down, according to Father O'Neil. More and more, he turned to his reading, and near the end he concentrated on books of religion.

It was thus that about six years before his death he came to Father O'Neil to begin instructions in becoming a Catholic. When the good priest explained the complications that would result from such a decision, and the impact it would have on his non-Catholic friends, Harry replied, "I don't give a goddamn! This is my decision!" That was the last time Father O'Neil ever heard Harry swear.

So Harry was received in to the Catholic faith long before the Ecumenical movement, and there was indeed bitterness in the community. Many of his friends shunned him entirely, with one prominent politician of the period telling Father O'Neil that Harry would use both him and the church, and wouldn't change his life-long beliefs. The good priest replied, "That's between Harry and God; and it was his decision, not mine."

When I asked Father O'Neil what had impressed Harry most about the Catholic faith he told me it dated back to the building of the Flin Flon Railway. He never forgot the dedication of the Oblate fathers working up North, who administered to the sick and the desolate. The way they slaved in poverty helped the desperate and the dying.

Then there was a Mother Superior of St. Francis Hospital in Smiths Falls, who he admired greatly. During his bouts with alcohol he had sought help in the best medical institutions of the day, but in none of them did he find the love he received at the little St. Francis Hospital.

When he entered the hospital, the little sister would take over completely – firmly but kindly – and sit with him for hours, as he fought through his first few days of withdrawal. Although Harry donated thousands to the hospital, he often said that he could never repay them in money for the kindness he received during these agonizing visits.

When the end came one blustering March day, Father O'Neil was with him. A requiem High Mass was held in St. Anne's Church in the little village, but few of the Ottawa politicians were there.

Yet I don't think Harry would have cared, for his real friends had come. The United Church Minister, Mr. Armstrong, nearly all of his former employees, Harry Durant, and Dick Preston; and, like they say, if you can count a dozen true friends in your life you're a lucky man. There were more than a dozen there that day at the funeral, but when he was buried in Notre Dame cemetery there were only seven: the undertaker, Dick Preston, Father O'Neil and his wife, Rita, with her two brothers.

So it was that Harry was buried in Montreal, in the city where his first wife rests, and where his second wife, Rita, now resides.

As I left Father O'Neil and made my way back to Toronto I thought of Margaret's words, "You know, money isn't everything." Then looking down on my car seat I glanced at a copy of Harry's will that had been probated in Surrogate Court in Brockville. No, money wasn't everything I thought, and nobody knew it better than Harry. For you see when he said his final goodbye he had only $75.62 in ready cash.

Yes, Harry's prayerbook was a little different than that of most people, but all railroaders will understand. He would lift his glass and boom forth a verse of Kipling's "Martha" – a prayer and tribute to the men of the road:

> *It is in their care in all ages*
> *To take the buffet and cushion the shock.*
> *It is in their care that the gear engages;*
> *It is in their care that the switches lock;*
> *It is in their care that the wheels run truly;*
> *It is in their care to embark and entrain,*
> *Tally, transport, and deliver duly,*
> *The sons of Martha by land and main.*

My kind of people 12

"Inquiry" Jack

A few years back I get a call from my friend, "Inquiry" Jack, and he tells me he's in Kingston, where he's just graduated from college. Now the only diploma that I know for sure Jack ever obtained was his sheepskin from the Dale Carnegie College. The accompanying document stated, among other things, that Jack had developed courage, effective speaking, leadership, and the ability of get along with others. On occasion, when he wished to put on the dog a bit, he would pull out his diploma, along with a poem he had written for the graduating class. Just so there will be no doubt regarding Jack's poetic ability, I'll give you one little verse:

> *Once I was bashful and ill at ease*
> *Couldn't converse without shaking knees*
> *Everything in me just seemed to freeze*
> *But now the words flow like the evening breeze.*

I had heard through the grapevine that Jack had been incarcerated for a spell, so I wasn't too surprised to learn he had been attending college. However, I was taken aback after enquiring what he had been studying this time, and he told me it had been theology. I hadn't known Jack was all that religious.

Jack was a French Canadian, who grew up in Maniwaki, Quebec. Some of his English friends called him a "frog," but Jack didn't mind. As a matter of fact, he rather took it as a compliment. When he'd get a snort too much he had this habit of shouting – right out of the blue:

> *Of all the fishes in the sea,*
> *The bull frog she's the fish for me!*

As you hear more about Jack, it may be a little hard for you to comprehend that he was ever very religious. He and his boyhood friend, Frenchy Richer, never missed Christmas midnight mass when they were living on the Quebec side of the border – at least – according to Frenchy. One Christmas, the two of them stood waiting in line to go to confession prior to the mass. Just in front of Jack was the tiny, pretty, cultured wife of a local, well-heeled politician. The little woman finally made her way into the confessional. Then the long wait began. Finally Jack turns to his friend Richer and says, "She must have shot her husband and Father won't give her absolution." After waiting another five minutes, Jack was really becoming impatient and he says to Frenchy, "She must have left the confessional by a hidden exit. I'm going in right now, or we'll be here all night."

In he went, and found himself kneeling on top of the pretty belle. All hell broke loose. Jack and the petite lady scrambled out one side of the confessional, landing on the floor, and Father Demers burst out of the other, utterly flabbergasted. Jack finally got to his feet and didn't stop running till he got to O'Reillys Hotel several blocks down the street.

But to get back to our phone conversation, Jack tells me that he's coming to Toronto for the Queen's Plate, and for me to meet him at the station. When I meet him, I get another big surprise. He's all decked out in a black suit and a clerical collar.

Right off, he asks me to take him to our lawyer, "Loophole" Montgomery's office, so he can arrange a little loan. We're sitting in the Loop's office, pouring a few drinks, when the heat seems to get to Jack a bit and he peels off his coat. Montgomery, never one to miss a trick, says, "I see you have your shirt on backwards." "Never mind that." answers Jack, "It's what you call putting on a front."

While Jack and Montgomery got down to personal business I left the office to sit in the waiting room, and got to thinking about the first time I ever met him. It was years ago, when I was a teenager. A fellow by the name of Morgan Mullville and I were having a morning drink in a graveyard on a side-road, north of the village of Westport. Now if you wonder why I was drinking on Eternity Hill – as Morgan called it – it wasn't my idea. He always claimed that there was no quieter or more peaceful setting in which to have a snort after a hard night than here with some quiet old friends. It not only gave one a chance to pay respects, but provided a setting where there was no back talk; nevertheless, it bothered him a bit that a lot of hopes lay buried here.

Anyhow, the two of us were seated behind the biggest tombstone in the place – a memoriam to one of the best-known bootleggers in the district also by the name of Murphy (although no relation). Suddenly the stillness was shattered by the arrival of a shiny, black Buick. Out jumped the township bailiff, Hilt, and another fellow I didn't know. Morgan however knew everybody, and he introduced the other fellow as "Inquiry" Jack. After we had shaken hands a couple of times, with a lot of back-slapping, Jack dispatched Hilt back to the car for some more refreshment. Then Jack got around to explaining why he was visiting the cemetery. He said that he'd been away from the district for the past couple of years. Arriving back, just a week previously, he had heard of old Murph's passing. Unfortunately, he had left this planet owing Jack quite a bundle. So Jack had engaged Hilt the bailiff to see if there were any remaining assets. Apparently, the only thing left of any value was this tombstone.

Jack went on to explain he hadn't been feeling all that well himself during the past ten years. He had just come down from Maniwaki, where he had purchased a burial plot, and had given Father Demers a tenner, just in case he should still be around for Jack's requiem. The only thing lacking was a tombstone. "But, by the looks of things," said Jack, gazing up at Murph's big monument, "I'm out of luck. We could never get it in the car, and it would cost too much to have it moved."

Well, Morgan was quite relieved to hear that, as he liked the stone where it was. Smiling wryly, he asked, "And what would an old reprobate like you want printed on the stone?"

Jack rubbed his chin. After a few minutes of deep reflection answered:

I never amounted to a hell of a lot
But I hope to hell I'm not forgot.

We spent the rest of the day recalling the different characters around the district, and it sure was quite a visit. Come nightfall, Jack said he had to be on his way. He explained that he didn't mind drinking in a cemetery, but now that he was feeling better he would rather not sleep there, so he and Hilt took off – minus Murphy's tombstone, I might add.

All during the visit I had noticed that Jack would use the expression, "That fellow couldn't tell you the number of balls in a male quartet," when he was describing someone he didn't exactly admire. Since the expression stuck in my mind a bit, I asked Morgan about it before we bedded down for the night. He explained that this was one of the many questions that Jack used to put to smart-alecky fellows. He went on to say it was impossible to come up with the correct answer unless you were there to hear the quartet sing. Well, being a little naive I said the answer seemed simple enough to me, and that if all were normal there would be a total of eight. "Could be," replied Morgan, "but then again there might be forty; one or all might be tenors."

So here I am, thirty years later, and Jack is still a long way from needing a tombstone. As I sat watching him through the half-open door to Montgomery's office I thought I'd never seen him look better. I watched as the Loop handed him a little currency, and I heard Jack telling him not to worry: the loan would be paid in full, and it was even insured if something ever happened to him, as Loop was the only benefactor in his will.

Finally Jack got up, and having put on his coat was about to leave, when he realized he had forgotten something. Turning to the Loop, he said, "I'd also appreciate it if you could give me a couple of streetcar tickets, as I don't like making change."

The two of us then headed out to Woodbine on the bus. On the way, I asked Jack if he intended to take up preaching full time. He replied that it might be a little tough for a fellow who had spent most of his life singing from a different hymn book than most other people. "You got to remember that many are called but few are chosen. I ain't exactly a born-again Christian, as I think that this is my ninth or tenth crack at it. In the meantime, I plan to make a few contacts and start peddling my new horse medicine."

Years ago, with the help of his friend, Dr. Rolly S., he had come up with a cure-all for sore horses which he called "Miracle Whip." I don't want you to get this concoction mixed up with the salad dressing of the same name, as Jack had gotten his idea from the old cowshit plaster – once a popular poultice for sore horses. By adding a few secret ingredients, it was his claim that the said medicine could be taken internally for various ailments. I don't recall all of Jack's sales pitch, but I do remember it ended with the words, "It's good for coughs, colds, sore holes, and pimples on the dink."

You see, against Dr. Rolly's advice, Jack had decided to branch out and market his product as a cure-all for humans as well. He ran an ad in the various Valley weeklies, which went something like this: "If you have trouble with a burning sensation, constipation, functional bladder weakness, disturbed sleep, dull pain in the back down through to the groin, then you should try our new wonder drug." At the bottom of the ad, he told all anguished sufferers to send two bucks to a post-box number in Arnprior.

Like many of Jack's friends, the only time I used the medication was when I was experiencing a burning sensation in my stomach after a hard night. I made sure he extracted my own personal medication from a barrel marked "additive only." The additive was the over-proof, that Jack, and his friend "the Gap," used to import from Montreal. The Gap got his name from the rather wide division between his two front teeth – or "the gap in his yap," as Inquiry put it. Gap was rather an obnoxious character who Jack described best as, "one of those fellows who was always pissing against the wind."

It is said that the Gap was one of the first in the Valley to ever wear a wig. It was fashioned from the tail of Toll Gate – one of the most famous race horses ever to grace a track in Eastern Ontario. However, when I knew him, he had long discarded this head-piece, and wore a black cap pulled down over both ears and most of his nose. The story goes that while partying one night at an outdoor camp meeting he began doing his famous war dance. Circling a bonfire, and stumbling, he lost the wig to the flames of the fire.

The incident became well-publicized locally, and it became the subject of one of Inquiry Jack's poems. Again, I am at a loss to remember all of it, except for the following lines:

> *The poor silly ass*
> *He fell on the grass*
> *While doing the jig*
> *He lost his wig*
> *If ever a rig*
> *Looked like a pig*
> *It had to be the Gap*
> *With his pulled-down cap.*

Well, the two of them were making their once-a-week excursion to Montreal, and on their return they would always disembark at the tiny station of Rosedale, two miles east of the Falls. Rosedale was a little outhouse of a station, tucked in the wilderness, almost hidden by dense bush. It was beyond the jurisdiction of the Smiths Falls police – at the time headed by Chief "Chesty" Philips – who took a dim view of illicit alcohol coming into the valley.

One night, as Inquiry and the Gap were about to disembark at the tiny station, they spied Chesty and two provincial officers standing on the platform. Jack handed all the booze to the Gap, and told him to stay on the train. They would meet later behind the freight sheds in Smiths Falls. He then gathered up his tiny terrier, Lippy – a constant companion. Tucking him under his overcoat, he climbed down to the station platform. Whether it was the long train ride, or the fact that he did not like to be confined, Lippy let go, and the dampness ran down Jack's sleeve. Chesty was right on the job. Accompanied by one of the Provincials, he walked over, and with finger extended wiped a few drops from Inquiry's sleeve. Tasting it, he said with a knowing smile, "That's gin!" "Like hell it is," said Jack. "That's dog piss!" With that, he opened his coat and let Lippy take a little stroll.

Needless to say, Chesty really had it in for Jack. Thereafter, to be on the safe side, Jack employed his girlfriend, Moonshine Molly, to make the Montreal run. Molly delivered the goods each week without mishap, until one cold night just before Christmas. She got off the train loaded down with shopping bags – a couple of months supply – and crossed the street to what is now the Lee Hotel, where Jack stood waiting. Right off, Chesty surmised something was going on when he saw Jack taking the bags from Molly. The chase began. Jack made rapid progress through a number of backyards, with Chesty in hot pursuit. Finally, he reached a yard that contained a pile of bricks. He grabbed one and let it fly. Chesty cried out in pain. The natural result was Jack being charged with assaulting a police officer. Fortunately, the old Magistrate was a little hard of hearing. After listening to a couple of hours of dragged-out testimony, he decided to get down to the basic facts, so he said to Philips, "What exactly did this man do to be charged with assault?" "He hit me with a brick," the good chief answered. "He called you a prick!" said the magistrate. "Well, that certainly wasn't very nice, but that's an insult, not an assault. Case dismissed!"

Well, I was certainly enjoying my reunion with Jack, and in no time at all we arrived at Woodbine. As we climbed down from the bus, Jack took a brush from his hip-pocket and began brushing off his suit. Then turning to be he said, "You know it's important to reserve one day of the year to mingle with the high and mighty, and to see and be seen."

When we got to the ticket booths there was quite a line-up, except for the "Will Call" window, so Jack ambled up to it, and asked the pretty young girl if she had reservations for Father Jack and friend. The poor girl searched and searched through her sheet. Finally, she asked, "What's your last name, Father?" "Never mind that," said Jack, "I don't want the Cardinal to know I'm here." So she waved us in.

Right away, I began to feel a bit uncomfortable mixing with all these people, in their top-hats and tails, until Jack put me straight. He explained that most of them were no different than us. "If the truth were known," he went on to say, "most of these people haven't got a pot to piss in or a window to throw it out."

We were a bit early for the first race, so we ambled down to the walking ring and took a seat near where the CBC crew had set up headquarters. Mike McGee was being introduced as Canada's racing authority, and Jack, turning to me with a disgusted look, said, "What kind of bunk is that? There's no such thing as an authority when it comes to horses. Only the horse himself knows what he's going to do on a given day, and there are times when *he* needs a little help."

He then told me about another type of medication which one of his college friends had come up with. It was called "Speed." Now I know you've heard of the Speed drugs on the street, but Jack's product was an entirely different ballgame. He claimed that this new medication would save a lot of slow horses from a life of labour, or, at worst, the glue factory. It was solely for slow horses; and his reasons for marketing such a product was strictly humanitarian.

Well, it was years later that I was told by some of my old racehorse friends that Jack's "Speed" was a product of the drug etorphine. In general, it usually had a rather soothing effect on both man and animals – except for horses. With them, it produced such get-up-and-go results that it made a real kangaroo out of many a slow horse. The best part of it all, there were no known tests for the drug. Thus, Jack was able to save many a steed from the glue-pot. It was always a sore point with him that he had never been awarded a plaque for his humane approach to slow steeds.

Anyhow, to get back to the track, the two of us were sitting – still visiting – when along came the racehorse priest, Father Hal Smith. A bit surprised, he looked at Jack, then back at me and said, "I see you're in good company today." So I introduced Jack as Monseigneur Jack from P.E.I., and I asked the Father if he'd heard about anything good on the card. He replied he'd had a bit of a tip on Royal Chocolate in the plate, and, if it kept on raining, he liked the off-track. Well, I guess from being a bit wet inside, this was the first that Jack and I had noticed it was coming down quite hard.

Jack proposed that we go inside to try to find a seat. Just as we enter the club house, a short balding fellow surrounded by four husky "Horsemen" pushed by on the way out. Jack stopped dead in his tracks, and grabbing my shoulder said, "Ain't that Harold Allmand's son, the old railroad master-mechanic's boy they used to call Yogi?" "Might be," I replied, "but I wouldn't recognize him without his hair. He went on to be in charge of the last college you attended. He's the Solicitor General now you know, Jack."

"Go up to him, and ask if he happens to have an extra seat. And kind of remind him of the time he and Ray Naud stole the railway hand-car off the old man to go to a dance in Perth." Well, I had to laugh at Jack remembering that incident after all these years. I went back out the door, and hailed Allmand, introducing myself amid the stares of the four "Horsemen" – who turned out to be members of Canada's finest. I told him the tip I had on Royal Chocolate, and also inquired about his father's health. He said this his father was now retired from the railway, and was sitting in the Royal box with Governor-General George Vanier.

I went back in and told Jack that it was indeed Allmand, but he was sitting with the Governor-General, and the box was a little crowded. "Why that cheapskate!" said Jack. "You'd think he'd have squeezed us in. I hope you told him to say hello to Vanier for me." I replied that I certainly had. So, lacking seats, we headed to the closest washroom – which wasn't all that crowded – and Jack produced an unopened jug.

Right off, we decided to pool all our money, and lay it down early on Royal Chocolate. All I had was ten, so I handed it over to Jack and he headed off to make the bet, while I found a resting place in an empty stall. Hours later, I was awakened by a track cop who told me they were closing the gates, and I'd better get on my way. "Who won the Plate?" I asked rather sheepishly. "Royal Chocolate by five," he answered, hurrying me toward the exit.

Here I was, miles from my rooming house, with no money, so I started to walk to the nearest bus stop, hoping the driver would take pity on me, when I remembered I always kept a spare ticket in my right sock. I stooped down, and came up with a roll of toilet paper and a fin. Written on the paper were the words, "Here's your ten. I didn't get it down. Shipping out to Finger Lakes with a bunch of the boys. See you, Jack."

Well, see me again he did, but it was two years later. One hot summer night I was lying in bed, attired in what was left of a pair of undershorts. It was one of these steaming August nights with nary a movement, inside or out. It was so quiet you could hear the worms crawling on the front lawn. Finally the heat and stillness bothered me to such a degree I decided I must converse with somebody, so I climbed out of bed, and getting down on my knees, started to talk a bit with the Lord.

Suddenly the door burst open and in walked my landlady, "Game-Leg" Ruby. Seeing me on my knees, she was so startled she went over on her good leg and landed on the floor. After I managed to hoist her to a sitting position she told me that I had a very important telephone call. So leaving Ruby resting on my bed I headed for the phone downstairs. Right off, when I lifted the receiver and hear the raspy voice, I knew it was Inquiry Jack.

"Meet me at the Orchard Park across from the Greenwood track tomorrow at noon, and you won't regret it," he said, in the way of a greeting. With that, he hung up. I climbed back up the steps to find Ruby dozing on my bed. So I went down to hers, which was a bit cooler – as it had an old fan circulating the hot air – and managed to doze off myself.

It's surprising what a little sleep will do. When I woke Ruby the next morning and got her on her feet, both legs seem to be as sound as a dollar. She asked me what the phone call was all about. I told her that a fellow named Bill Stinson, who used to be around Smiths Falls a bit, had just been appointed General Manager of the CPR and he wanted to appoint me as his assistant. Although I then owed Ruby six month's rent, she was so happy to hear the news that she gave me twenty dollars and a couple of streetcar tickets. So I headed out to the east end.

I recognized Jack as soon as I walked in, although this time he was dressed more like a cowboy, with a string-tie and a big western hat. Sitting beside him was a little wrinkled-up fellow he introduced as the "Needle." After a little visit, he got down to business. He told me that he had been living outside of Albany, New York, had a stable of five trotters, and had been doing quite well – up until now, at least. He then went on to explain that the powers-that-be were after him and the Needle, concerning a little filly they had run in Saratoga. It seemed that the Needle had administered a little of Jack's "Help" to the filly – which won rather easily – and the two of them had made quite a bundle. The stewards, however, were a little suspicious and they ordered a test, but the filly was flying so high it took a couple of days to bring her down. Although the test proved negative, Jack was still under investigation, so he and his friend had come up to the Valley for a little holiday.

He said they had spent a couple days around Smiths Falls, but things were not the same, as all the old bunch had passed away except Cowboy Curran, who was racing the Toronto circuit, and would be in town tonight. The Cowboy had a horse going in the Seventh – the best of a bad lot – except for the one Ron Feagan would be driving. "In the same race," Inquiry went on to say, "there is a lady named Greta driving the number three horse – which we will call White Satin – and this being her birthday, the boys are going to let her win. That's where you come in," he then explained. "Since the Needle and I can't shine shoes within a mile of a track till things are cleared up, I've raised four hundred smackers that I want you to lay on Greta. There'll be a healthy commission for you, as I always felt you might be a little perturbed about that deal we had at the Queen's Plate." Well, since it was all Jack's money I felt I had nothing to lose, so I agreed to meet him at the same location right after the race.

I headed straight to Montgomery's office for a little financial advice, and let him in on the deal. Finally, after a lot of brain-searching, the Loop said that since he was solicitor to both Inquiry and myself, maybe it would be wise if *he* made the investment. So I gave him Jack's four hundred, along with Ruby's twenty, and told him I'd meet him after the race, just outside the main gate.

I left for the track early, so I could walk in free with the cleaning staff, then waited around until nearly ten, when the seventh race was to begin. I watched Greta warming up White Satin, and never saw a trotter look better. Cowboy's horse, the long shot on the board, looked a little washed out, as did Ronny Feagan's. As for the rest of the field, I didn't pay much attention. When the race began, everything was as Jack predicted. Greta immediately took the lead. Coming for home, White Satin had an open lead of six with about a hundred yards from the wire. Then it happened. I'll be damned if Satin didn't break, and who whizzes by but Cowboy Curran.

I was heartbroken. I knew that this was one night that not even the Loop would be talking to me. It was a long walk from the track to Ruby's rest home, but there was no way I was going to face the Loop and his driver, Joe Hibbs. So I began my sorrowful journey. I had gotten about twelve blocks down the street from the track when I heard a horn honking, and a car pulled up. It was the Loop and Hibbs, so I climbed in the back seat with my head down, wishing they had passed me by. The last thing I needed was a blast from the Loop.

For what seemed an eternity, there was complete silence. Then Montgomery finally turned and asked, "How come you're so down-hearted?" As if he didn't know. It wasn't until the three of us were seated at Dooley's bar out in the west end that Montgomery was to give me the best financial advice I ever had. To begin with he said,

"Who do you trust? An honest man or a rogue? The Cowboy or the likes of Inquiry Jack? *I* believed in the Cowboy, and I put all the money on him."

What did he pay to win?" I asked, almost falling off the bar stool. "Fourteen even," he replied, handing me a hundred dollars. "What about the other forty you owe me, and the twenty-eight hundred of Jack's?" I asked, feeling a little braver now.

"Well, your forty is my commission. And Jack's twenty-eight hundred is a down payment on what he owes me."

All lawyers are a bit expensive, so I passed it off, and asked if he would mind giving me a little free advice. I told him that I owed Ruby for three month's rent, and would I be wise to give her fifty of my winnings? He went into another thinking spell and finally advised that I pay her only ten, as it was better that I owe her at least two month's rent at all times.

"It works like this," he explained. "If you owe the bank a thousand dollars, then you're in trouble, but if you own them a million *they're* in trouble." In the meantime, he advised me to buy a round for a change.

Well, that was the last I ever saw or heard tell of Inquiry Jack. Some say he passed away in Albany, and was returned to be buried in an unmarked plot near "Murph's" on Eternity Hill. Maybe so, but nobody knows for sure. So it is thus I pay tribute to an old friend who made my life a little richer in more ways than one. Hello to you Jack wherever you are. Like me, you may not have amounted to a hell of a lot, but I assure you, my friend, you're not forgot.

Boarding-House Life: "Game-Leg" Ruby and Other Interesting Characters

It was a typical business meeting for my friend, Long John Maclean, and me. We had entered the old Prince George Hotel on King Street and waited in the lobby for Mike the bartender to open our office, sharp at noon. We would then proceed to our desk, the second table down from the door in the beverage room.

Maclean would be attired in his striped double-breasted business suit, well-pressed but a little shiny. Adorning the top of his pinhead was a brown scout-master's hat, a symbol, I guess, of his present occupation – selling apples on Bay Street.

The John Maclean had been a newspaper legend who worked the old *Toronto Telegram* for years. His exploits would fill a book. He knew a good story, and made many of them himself. His days on the *Tely* had come to an end when he had stowed away on the aircraft carrier, *Magnificent*, which was taking the U.N. troops to the Middle East at the time of the Suez war. He was caught hiding in a lifeboat, armed with a portable typewriter, his camera, a hundred cheese sandwiches, and a case of booze. As Peter Worthington was to say, some years later, when he wrote a farewell column on Maclean's untimely death: "This was too much for the razzle-dazzle *Tely*, but as long as there are those who call themselves 'reporters,' not 'journalists' or 'writers,' Harrison John Maclean will live forever."

On this particular day we had just been seated, when we were joined by Hughy Garner, whose *Liberty Magazine* had just folded, and police reporter Little Billy McGuire, whose paper, the *Tely*, was getting ready to fold. The fifth chair was soon to be taken by Jack Humphrey who was on assignment, but was later to write the television series *King of Kensington*.

Of the five sitting at the table, McGuire and I were the only two gainfully employed. I had found a seven-night-a-week job from twelve till eight in the morning. My work consisted of tending a boiler on Parliament Street, where on arrival I would bank the firebox with coal, fill the boiler to overflowing with water, then lie down behind the coal bin and sleep away the night. I always managed to come to an hour before the chief engineer arrived to get the place in order for the day shift. Being well-rested, I spent my mornings wandering about until the "Office" opened at noon.

Somehow, the first order of business on this particular day was the importance of me finding a room. Maclean had long argued that a man of my status should have a mailing address and a place to hang his clothes. Well, I may have needed a mailing address, but I certainly didn't need a place to hang my clothes. My total wardrobe consisted of two pairs of coveralls, one of which I wore on social and business occasions, such as this, and the other pair, which served as pyjamas, I left on the job.

After a little discussion, McGuire began scanning the ads and finding nothing suitable for a man of my standing, handed the paper to Maclean, who removed a pair of field-glasses from around his neck and began scanning the ads. At the moment I have forgotten whether or not Maclean was wearing the field-glasses on this occasion, due to the fact he had lost his spectacles, or that he believed they went well with his boy-scout hat. I do know he spent many a night peering through their lenses at the great beyond.

Finally he spotted an ad which he felt met the requirements. It read in part: LARGE CHRISTIAN HOME HAS A VACANCY FOR A SOBER CULTURED GENTLEMAN PREFERABLY A NON-SMOKER. It gave the location, 54 Madison Avenue – an address of which John assured me I would be proud, as it was in the heart of the University of Toronto district.

As was the custom in those days, our office, like all beverage rooms in Ontario, was closed down for an hour at six o'clock to allow the patrons to go for supper and get a little lining in their stomachs for the evening sessions. It was thus Maclean and I headed for the Madison Avenue address, where we rang the doorbell several times to no avail. Finally we entered the unlocked door, to find a little old toothless lady sleeping peacefully in a rocking chair. We were later to learn her name was Auntie, but in a few short months that I knew her, I never heard her first or last names.

Maclean was able to rouse Auntie by tickling her nose with a feather he had extracted from his scouting hat. Auntie awoke with a smile, and although a little hard of hearing, finally realized what we were after. She pointed to a closed door across the hall and said, "Ruby's in there."

Rapping at the door we again received no answer, so opening it a crack we peered in, to find another lady of questionable age lying half and half out of the bed, with a bible resting on her lap. The squeaking door must have roused her a bit, as she turned her head and said out of the side of her mouth, "What is it you want?" Maclean explained why we had come, and Ruby, peering at me from eyes which were encased by long droopy lids which never opened more than a hair, lay gazing at me for what seemed like hours. Finally she said, "I have one room left in the basement. The one I advertised isn't available. Go down those back steps," she pointed, "and you'll find a fellow named Sam who'll show the room." With that her eyes disappeared again entirely, and after giving a couple of grunts, she appeared to fall back into a deep slumber.

When the two of us reached the bottom step of the darkened dungeon, Maclean began hollering, "Sam, where the hell are you?" Finally a light appeared in the darkness, not unlike a train rounding a bend in a tunnel, and beneath it chugged the tiniest of humans with the craggiest face I had ever seen. The miner's light mounted on his head revealed little of his body – only the face. As the light shone less than four feet above the floor, you knew right away that Sam was short, to say the least. "If it's worms you want I ain't got any. It snowed all night." was his greeting.

We assured him that we had not come for worms but to rent a room. So he told us to follow him. Making a turn he started back through the tunnel from whence he had come, with his miner's lamp lighting the way. Finally we reached the furnace room, which Sam said was his abode. It was rather sparsely furnished but, as the Worm Picker was later to say, it's hard to design the proper décor for a room with a big coal-fired furnace stuck in the middle. There were however, two broken-down chairs, a bed, and several cans of worms which lay by the side of the furnace – sharing Sam's hospitality and warmth from outside forces.

When Maclean and I were seated, Sam went over to the only other piece of furniture – a trunk pushed in the corner – extracted an over-size key from his pocket, opened it a crack and pulled out a bottle of Old Sailor – our favourite brew. Right away we knew we had found a friend. After an hour or two of getting acquainted, Sam explained in detail the set-up of Ruby's Rest Home.

Now, I am not going to paraphrase his entire conversation but, in short, he informed us that Ruby, who had one game leg – and was none too sound on the other – was a rather strict landlady. She was a Christian lady, as the ad in the paper had implied, a former Presbyterian who had turned to the more evangelical form of religion. She now placed her trust in faith healers, hoping that the Lord would restore her pins. At heart, Sam explained, she was still a good Presbyterian, who allowed no drinking or any other immoral activities on the premises. The rules, however, did not apply strictly to the basement. It seems that the last time Ruby climbed down the long narrow basement steps, her undercarriage had given out, and it had taken four of them to get her back up to her room. As a result, she had little contact with any of the dungeon tenants, except old bald-headed Jim, who had been an admirer of hers for years.

For the past two years, Sam went on to explain, Ruby had not much truck with Jim romantically, but as he was a non-drinker, and had a car, she gave him free room and board in exchange for his services as her chauffeur. He also collected the basement rents and gave Ruby a daily report of the goings-on in the basement. The Worm Picker gave me advance warning not to trust Jim.

As for his own relationship with Jim, Sam let us in on a little secret. It seemed that since Ruby had begun to shun his romantic advances, Jim had turned his attention to Auntie, who nightly retired just after supper, to her second-floor bedroom. Ruby had assigned him the job of helping Auntie up the steps to her room. The good part of all this was that Jim never returned after these trips of mercy, so we didn't have to worry about him after seven in the evening.

Now right away Maclean and I were a little taken aback, as this was long before the Kinsey Report, and having seen Auntie we knew she was no chicken. So we inquired about Jim's age, and were informed that he was in his middle seventies.

As Sam talked on I began feeling more and more comfortable, sensing that this was indeed the type of lodging that I was looking for, and I decided right away to take the room next to Sam and his furnace. Maclean advised that it would be wise to take the night off work, move in and become acclimatized. I mentioned that I'd have to make a phone call to my employer, and Sam responded, "That's no problem." Again he went to his trunk, extracted the most ancient phone I've ever seen, and skilfully hooked it to Ruby's line. After listening a minute or two, to see that he had a clear line, he told me that I could make my call.

This accomplished, Maclean called me to one side to tell me that since first impressions were important, it might be wise for me to present a little front. So excusing ourselves, Maclean explained to Sammy that we must pick up my belongings from my present address, down at the Royal York Hotel.

With that, we left Sammy after receiving a key, and wandered down Madison along Bloor to Spadina till we reached the Dominion Store. Going to the back of the store, we picked up five empty cardboard boxes, filled them with paper, and headed back to Ruby's Rest Home.

Well, when Sam heard us at the back door, he turned on the lights, and discarded his miner's cap. Right away he was impressed by all my luggage, and offered to help carry it to the room. Maclean however insisted that it was too heavy. When we got things arranged in my room, we joined Sammy for another little visit.

The Worm Picker informed us that his supply of Sailor was getting low, but in an hour or so a fresh supply would be arriving. It was then he told us about the two other tenants in the basement. They were two brothers from P.E.I., Laughing Louie and Honest Jack. Louie worked at a car-wash up on Dupont Street and Jack, the younger, was weighed down by a plate in his head, the result of falling off a box car during his early days of travel and adventure.

At the moment he was unemployed, and was acting as house bus-boy, running errands for any roomer needing his services. His present assignment was that of replenishing Sam's trunk with more Old Sailor.

Sam explained that they would be arriving shortly after nine – when the wine store just up the street on Bloor closed. He warned that their arrival might be a little noisy, as like Ruby, they always fell down the steps, rather than coming down the more conventional way. Unlike Ruby, however, the fall had little effect, and both would be on their feet in no time.

Just as Sam had warned, there was a bit of a commotion a few minutes later, then a silence, followed by footsteps outside the Worm Picker's door. Laughing Louie and Honest Jack had arrived. They were both loaded down (in more ways that one) with brown paper bags, which they placed gently on Sam's trunk.

It was a marvellous get-to-know-you party. It lasted all night, and right through until the next night, when I realized I was due on my job by twelve. I gave Clinker Bill a call on Sam's phone and told him to go home, and that I would be on the job in half an hour. But I guess the partying had caught up with me, because I lay down in my room, waiting for Jack the messenger to return with the evening refreshment, and I slept through until ten the next morning, when a long pounding at the door woke me. Who should be standing there but Ziggy, the owner of the company for which I worked. Next, there was a crash, as Ziggy fell flat on the floor. Now there were mornings when I didn't look any too good, but never so bad that it would cause anybody to die of shock.

Sammy, hearing the commotion, ran for a pail of water and doused poor Ziggy like he was on fire. Finally Ziggy got groggily to his feet, clutching a folder that I recognized as my company insurance policy – which I always kept in an old desk drawer in the boiler room with my one other valuable – an alarm clock. When Ziggy was finally back on his feet he revealed what had caused his collapse.

It seems that the boiler had blown up some time during the night, taking most of the building with it, and it was generally believed I, too, had exploded. Someone had told Ziggy I roomed at this address, so he came with the insurance policy to locate my benefactor, Garfield Franklin Montgomery.

I explained that Garfield, or "Loophole," was my attorney, and

I would get Sam to make a personal call to arrange an appointment. In the meantime I said I didn't wish to discuss anything until we met with Loop. I told him he could sit down and have a drink of wine. He replied that he did need a drink, so Honest Jack was dispatched to the closest liquor store for a bottle of Crown Royal (at Ziggy's expense).

After a couple of snorts he got real friendly, and told me that he was glad in a way that the building had gone up, as it was getting pretty ancient. It was well insured, so well in fact that he might make quite a bundle. Then Sam returned, to tell us he had made contact with the Loop, and we could see him at twelve noon sharp in his office on Bloor Street. We got there punctually, and I told Loop what was going on. I then explained that, since I was presumed dead, and he was to collect the money, it might be a good idea for me to remain hidden for a spell at Ruby's – since I was quite comfortable – and he could collect the insurance and give me a couple of thousand.

Montgomery was having none of that however, and told me, in the harshest of tones, that I was asking him to commit fraud. Then, turning to Ziggy, he said, "Since I'll be the only benefactor of this terrible misfortune, I would advise that you give Murphy the face-value of the policy in cash, so there will be no insurance investigation." Ziggy thought for a moment and agreed this might be the solution. He arranged for the said money to be delivered, in my name, to Montgomery's office the next morning.

Thus began my first year of leisure, staying at Ruby's Rest Home, entertaining my writer and artist friends, and passing myself off as heir to a large estate. But before all of this – and on the day after the money had been delivered – Maclean advised that I would be wise if I held a wake. My own wake, so that a lot of my friends who might not see another winter, might attend to pay their respects – not only to me, but to each other. So for three days and nights we held the wake with Sam – who had been partying a little too much – representing the corpse. During the whole ceremony, he only came to once in a while to go to the bathroom, or gulp down the odd glass of Old Sailor. Like his worms, he kind of hibernated for a spell.

It was only a couple of months later when misfortune reached out with an ugly hand to plague the house with tragedy. Maclean, Garner, and I were sitting in on a business meeting in my room when we heard a terrible banging on the water pipes. Now the banging on pipes was a pre-arranged signal between Sam and Ruby, and it meant that something was wrong upstairs. If the banging was really intense it signalled an emergency, and required Sam's immediate attention, so he came to my room and asked the three of us to accompany him.

When we got upstairs Ruby was in a panic. She said, "It's Auntie, go quick to the second floor." The four of us raced to Auntie's room, to find her lying on what remained of a broken bed, in deep pain but still with a trace of a smile on her face. Jim in his long underwear was standing over her, along with two girls from the next room, Thelma and Nancy. Immediately Maclean, always the reporter, began taking down the particulars from the two attractive college coeds. If Maclean were alive today, I'm sure he could give you a better account, but to make it brief, Nancy stated that she and Thelma were studying when they heard Auntie shouting, "Easy, easy!" Then there was a hell of a crash and a lot of painful moaning.

Right away, Sam wasn't fooled by Auntie's smiling, so he ran downstairs and called for an ambulance. Poor Auntie, she only lived for a couple of days. They buried her a few days later. And damn that Jim, he never even showed up for the funeral. Maclean had to rent a car and do the chauffeuring. On the way to the graveyard, which was down near Port Hope, Ruby broke down for the first time and mumbled, "Auntie was a good Christian woman – if it wasn't for her weakness for men." Gradually however her sorrow subsided and she muttered under her breath, "Thank God the poor soul was well-insured."

Well, Ruby's basement became a much better environment with Jim the Snitch gone and Ruby's finances in better shape. The rules became a little more relaxed. Up until then, there had been no females allowed to visit the basement. This however was to change. One night I ways lying in bed reading the daily paper when one of the most beautiful girls I have ever laid eyes on came to the door. "Hi," she said in broken English, "I'm Olga the artist and I have come to paint your door." Well I must say it took me aback somewhat, but the door did need painting and I needed the company.

Right away I reached under my pillow and asked her if she cared for a little grape. Smiling prettily she refused, and softly said, "I never drink – just smoke." It was then I noticed that between her lovely lips was the longest cigarette holder I had ever seen, and dangling from its end was a homemade cigarette which smelled like the green tea I used to smoke as a kid. This was my first introduction to "grass," and although I had never used it myself, I was to learn through some of Olga's later escapades that it could be quite potent, for some at least!

Now as Olga started her painting – stooping over and beginning at the bottom of the door – I noticed she was clad only in a mink coat which barely covered her behind. To put it bluntly, I made a little pass. She turned quickly and landed one on my jaw, with the warning, "Let me be!" That was the last pass I ever made at my new friend, although I spent many a night in her company. Olga explained that she was putting a base paint on the door, and when it dried she'd be back to perform her work of art – with the door as her canvas. I could hardly wait for her return, but it didn't take place till a couple of nights later.

In the meantime I had the Worm Picker inquire around. He came back with the news that Olga was Swedish, and had come to Canada under the sponsorship of a rich grandmother to pursue – or should I say, "round out" – her career at the College of Art. Grandma was forwarding quite a large stipend to pay for Olga's education and rather lavish tastes. It was also disclosed that Olga's grandmother spent a year in Canada, learning English, and had slipped Ruby a few dollars to keep an eye on her pride and joy.

The night Olga finally made her second appearance, Maclean, Garner, the Worm Picker and I were having a late-night meeting. In she walked, with her usual "Hi!" – attired in her fur jacket.

Right away she began to paint, starting again at the bottom of the door. All eyes were on Olga – not her painting. Finally the Worm Picker broke the silence with the words, "Oh my, oh my, ain't that something!" Olga turned and said to Sam, "You like, little man?" Sam sheepishly nodded, with his eyes fixed this time on the numerous lines and circles which were unfolding on the door.

Olga went back to work in silence and Maclean and Garner began discussing their opinions on art. Sam and I were contented to view the lines of Olga. Meanwhile, the discussion became rather deep. It began, I think, about the difference between a painter and an artist. The two of them finally came to the conclusion that Michelangelo was an artist and the Group of Seven – two members of which they knew quite well – were painters.

As Olga progressed, Garner seemed deeply impressed exclaiming, "Look at those lines! Although I don't know what they mean, like all great artists, she leaves so much to the imagination." Even Sam and I, with our limited knowledge, had to agree on that.

Maclean, not taking a back seat to Garner, said, "She has a great ability to capture light. Maybe it helps if you're lit."

It was close to eight the next morning when Olga completed her mural. She turned and asked rather sweetly if there was a bath in the basement. Sam immediately informed her there was, and told her he would prepare the tub and draw the water. Turning to the three of us who remained sitting in awe of her work she said, "I have just cleansed the inside of me and now I start on the outside." With that, she jumped into the bathtub, fur coat and all.

When Olga retired to her room, leaving a pool of water which had dripped from her coat and her long blonde hair, and looking like a half-drowned rat as she disappeared, the four of us sat speechless. The silence was finally broken by Garner: "Gentlemen, hanging on that door is a masterpiece of cryptic art. Now if you don't know what that means don't feel bad." I didn't either, until Maclean was later to explain that "cryptic" means "secret"; thus, on my door hung the hidden secrets of Olga's troubled mind.

The Worm Picker and I were later gazing at the spectacle of the many coloured lines, circles and curves – a background for little demons appearing in all directions – when Sam uttered an opinion that we both shared, "If that's what's inside of me, I'd rather leave it there. But the door does look better."

Gradually, all four walls of the room became murals of Olga's cryptic art. Like a thief in the night, she'd perform her miracles. The only part of her that lingered when I awoke in the morning was the potent, burnt-tea smell. Finally, one afternoon when I lay resting on my bed, Olga appeared at the door loaded down with clothing. In her arms was a new blue suit, white shirt, red tie, and a pair of black shoes, even socks and underwear.

"Every Sunday night," she said in the way of greeting, "you dine with Olga. Have a bath first." Thereby began my summer of high society. Olga and I would visit the most plush Yorkville restaurants for nights of candlelight and wine. As for the other six nights of the week, I lived on stew from a pot that simmered on the Worm Picker's stove twenty-four hours a day. It wasn't your ordinary stew, as it was well fortified with the most choice hunks of beef you ever hung a lip over. The meat came from Ruby's pot, which she left simmering every Monday while she did the shopping. It was Honest Jack, the messenger's, job to go up and fish out the finer cuts of meat while she was gone. He would then replace them with a few potatoes. As Ruby was feeding eight boarders at the time, I presume the substitute was at least filling.

Life for the most part was unfolding as it should. I was eating well and drinking even better. All visitors to my new art gallery were charged an admittance fee equal to the value of a bottle of Old Sailor. Believe me, there were many visitors. Sundays were, however, the days I looked forward to the most. I'd have my bath at four in the afternoon and change into my new blue suit, then wait in readiness for Olga to take me out on the town.

One Sunday I was sitting all decked out waiting for Olga, when in came Maclean. Right off he remarked how well and distinguished I looked. I let him in on my little secret, and it was then he came up with a suggestion. Now, some of Maclean's suggestions could get a fellow in a lot of trouble. As it turned out, this happened to be one of them. He proposed that I ask Olga that very night for a more meaningful relationship. I'm sorry to say, I took his advice.

We were sitting at a dark candlelit table, when I reached over and gently held Olga's hand mumbling something about it was time we had a more meaningful relationship. Right away and rather loudly she began putting things in perspective. If anybody was having a meaningful relationship, she began, it had to be me. She was spending almost a hundred a week on entertaining me, let alone buying me clothes and lending me the odd fin when I was a little short. That was the last time I ever heard Olga raise her voice in my presence, and the last time I might add, that I asked for any change in our relationship.

Like all good things, however, it had come to an end. One night Honest Jack and I were returning home when we spotted the Fire Department parked in front of our house. As we stood on the front lawn, wondering what was going on, out came a stretcher bearing Olga and her fur coat.

It seems that she had been taking a bath, left the water running, and had fallen asleep. She had swallowed a little water and almost drowned. Ruby, true to her word, phoned Sweden. The next day, Granny arrived and made preparations for Olga to go back home with her.

It was one of the saddest days of my life when the air limousine arrived to pick up Olga and her Grandmother. Maclean had rented a Hertz truck to take Olga's trunk. He and I were sitting in the cab of the truck, with Worm Picker, Laughing Louie, and Honest Jack in back with Olga's luggage, as we made our way to the airport.

When Olga reached the plane's ramp she turned, and throwing her arms around my neck said, "I'll be back sometime, Mike, when I'm really clean inside." Then, pulling me closer whispered, "Olga miss you." My eyes filled with tears, and I started to walk away. Maclean, who had been standing back in silence, caught up with me. "I guess it was a more meaningful relationship than any of us thought," he said, as we headed towards the truck.

As the four of us stood by the truck, watching the plane disappear in the northern sky, the Worm Picker, who didn't look at all happy mumbled, "At least we'll remember her going up, not down. She'll never fly higher than that."

The weeks that followed were days of mourning. But life must go on. Maclean proposed that I take over Jim's old job as chauffeur, and move upstairs to Auntie's room, as my gallery room was too much of a reminder of the past. So began my long climb up life's social ladder.

After Olga's departure, it became a summer of change around Ruby's Rest Home. The basement was almost entirely closed down, except for special social events. The Worm Picker, who somehow in his busy life had managed to father three sons, began receiving the Old Age pension. He went to live with his favourite – or Number One Son as he called him – so I didn't see a great deal of him. Laughing Louie and Honest Jack headed back to P.E.I., where they had inherited the family farm. The last I heard of them they were doing quite well, thank you.

As for Garner and Maclean they didn't show up very often either. Garner wrote a couple of successful novels and Maclean took a steady job with Southam Press. He also wrote a book about his discovery of the *Griffen* – the ship of Sieur de la Salle – which he figured had been hi-jacked for its cargo of furs. Historians claim that the *Griffen* is still missing, but some of those historians have been known to be wrong, too, you know. If Maclean said that the old wreck he found was the *Griffen*, that's good enough for me. I suppose it's possible for anyone to make an error of identification on anything lost for three hundred years, but even Rolly Murphy, the old naval artist, agreed with Maclean. If Rolly's knowledge of ships was anywhere close to his ability to bake bread on an outside oven, then there is no question that Maclean's discovery was indeed legitimate.

There's also no doubt Maclean had quite an imagination – which far surpassed that of anyone I ever met – except Brendan Behan. One time, again on the advice of Maclean, I had entered a drying-out joint down on Queen Street. Who should arrive late one night to occupy the other bed in the room but Behan. He had become a little too boisterous at one of his presentations here in the city, and the powers that be thought it might be wise if he cut down a couple of nights on his intake.

Like me at the time, Behan had no intention of giving up the grape. In no time the two of us were formulating a grand scheme to obtain a little joy juice. As I was a little better acquainted with the joint than Behan, it was left to me to come up with a bottle.

Now there was an Irish nurse in the place who we'll call Bridgette. I'd been watching her for a couple of nights, and was sure that she, too, was tippling a bit. It takes one to know one! So on the second night of Behan's stay, when the nurse had left her station, I slipped over to her desk and retrieved a full bottle of rye.

I'll never forget Behan laughing, as we sat at the window the next morning, watching Bridgette cross the street below on her way home. She had her nursing cap cocked to the one side of her head, and one of her white stockings hanging around her ankle like a bandage. I guess she'd brought an extra bottle – just in case.

Well, Behan decided then and there that his next play would be about our friend Bridgette; but I guess he never did get around to it. As a matter of fact, I don't think he ever returned to Canada. I heard from him only once after that. It was three in the morning when I got a collect call from New York. Behan wanted to know if I had a bottle. I explained to him that I'd have no problem finding one, but might run into a little difficulty getting it delivered.

Back at the roominghouse, Ruby was slowing down a bit each day, spending most of the time lying in bed listening to her religious programs on both radio and T.V. Although she still cooked meals for eighteen roomers – mostly students – other household chores were going from bad to worse. She therefore decided to advertise for help. The ad was again for a Christian gentleman, but stated on this occasion that room and board would be free if the chosen applicant pitched in to help with household chores.

Thus it was that Laurie the Butler appeared on the scene. The Butler was a Finn who, after landing in Halifax, had spent several years working on a farm. Deciding that there must be a better way of making a living, he came to Toronto to seek fame and fortune.

The Butler had arrived at Union Station on the back of a coal tender of a C.N. passenger train, and during all the years I knew him – twenty-four to be exact – he never did get the coaldust out of the lines of his wrinkled face or the back of his abbreviated neck. It was always Ruby's contention, however, that the Butler was as clean as a whistle, as he always washed his hands before handling food or eating utensils. Mrs. Hutton, a rather stuffy elderly roomer, thought differently. She didn't believe that all the dirt in the dishwasher had come from the dishes.

Laurie's vocabulary was quite limited when he arrived at Madison Avenue. It consisted of three words, "God bless you." If you gave him hell for something or other he would reply with a smile and the same three words, "God bless you."

In any event the Butler took over many of the household chores. He washed the dishes after every meal, and swept the dirt under the beds in the students' rooms, giving the place a tidy look. He also took on many of the responsibilities left undone since the departure of the Worm Picker and Honest Jack.

Gradually he learned a few more words of English – in a rather limited vocabulary – but he loved to visit. He'd come to my room to sit by the hour, and go on and on about something or other. I'd nod my head in agreement, and he'd smile happily, continuing his ramblings. Since he talked in a low voice, it made little difference whether I was writing or watching television. As long as I nodded my head every once in a while in acknowledgement, he seemed quite content.

Soon, Ruby promoted him to the job of chef. But this was clearly a mistake. Families who had sent as many as five children to board with Ruby, while they studied at various colleges in the city, were beginning to have second thoughts, due to the numerous complaints the children were raising at home. Ruby's reputation was indeed slipping, and gradually the student population diminished, to be replaced by what Ruby called riff-raff.

These were the Flower Children of the Sixties, who came in droves to Yorkville. They invaded all the rooming houses in the district.

Finally, Ruby realized that she could no longer put up with such trash, and she up and sold the house – lock, stock and barrel – deciding that she would live a life of leisure. She shopped around for a quiet neighbourhood, finally deciding on the west end of the city, at Indian Grove. By now, she had become quite dependent on the Butler, so she raised his weekly stipend to twenty dollars, and stipulated he would have a home for life if he remained in her employ.

As for me, I had finally found a full-time job. But she also invited me to go along, and continue as her part-time chauffeur. The house on Indian Grove was quite large, and when the three of us had settled in, Ruby realized that there were four bedrooms unoccupied. Never one to pass up a little extra income, she again inserted her ad. This time it was for retired Christians, wanting to partake in the comforts of a home, with all the trimmings, such as good meals and a pleasant atmosphere.

In no time at all the four rooms were occupied. The first to arrive was Gramma, an elderly Scottish woman, who at one time had run a rooming house herself. Gramma was to remain for years; but she was only a boarder for one day, when she decided, as I had a few years previously, to do her own cooking. The next to arrive was Dr. Rebecca Campbell, a former chiropractor, who became quite a close companion to Ruby. Through her knowledge, she had Ruby up and around, and hopping quite soundly on one foot. Then came the elderly spinster, Miss Hubble – quite pert in her lace and white gloves, which she always wore, even while sleeping. It seems that she had a thing about germs, and felt protected from any invasion by the gloves. The last to arrive was Dr. Wiggins, a tiny, stern little man with the shakes.

Now I don't want you to up and think that Doc's shakes were caused by too much indulgence in Old Sailor, as I was first led to believe. In truth, he was suffering from Parkinson's disease. He was however know to take the odd shot, and he and I spent many a pleasant hour at my new office – the Rondun Hotel on Roncesvalles Avenue.

The Doc had been a G.P. in various towns and cities throughout Eastern Canada. Then, after graduating in surgery, he somehow ended up in Chicago. Most of his work in the Windy City was confined to very private operations: removing bullets from mob members during the Dirty Thirties. Now Doc was a bit of a ladies' man, right up until the end. He had a smile that could melt the heart of the toughest of the fairer sex. I think it was Doc's smile that got him into trouble with the mob. He became a little too friendly with one of the gangster's girlfriends, and was given a one-way ticket to Montreal. This may have been the beginning of Doc's shakes. Due to his illness, he gave up his practice in medicine and became a consulting analyst. How successful he was at this he never said, but he certainly did a fair job of analyzing me, Ruby, and the rest of the roomers.

Doc was blessed with two fine sons, and a daughter who's now an actress in the Soaps, and lives in the Catskills. Another son, Louie, he had put down as a lost cause. As he said, Louie was a lot like me. He explained that Louie had gone to law school, but unable to wait to be called to the bar had begun practicing law ahead of time. As a result, he was neither called nor chosen. At that time, he was unemployed, and Doc said he would be honoured if I would introduce him to my lawyer friend, Loop Montgomery, who might provide him with some kind of a position in the legal profession.

Well, it just so happened that the Loop was in need of a title-searcher, so he told me to send Louie around. That was the last time Montgomery was ever able to contact Louie when he needed him. The only searching that took place consisted of Montgomery looking for Louie. Ruby was not all that fond of Louie either, as he generally showed up at mealtime, and neither he nor Doc contributed financially towards the extra mouth. Why she didn't see Louie's presence as a compliment I'll never know. He was one of the few people who gulped down Laurie's cooking and asked for a second helping.

Anyhow, Doc settled in at Ruby's and seemed to enjoy it very much. Every evening, he and I would stroll over to the Rondun Hotel for a few, and we'd no sooner be seated at our table when Bill the waiter would drop a bottle of beer in front of Doc. The good Doctor would take out a plastic straw, curved at right angles, and drain the bottle dry.

During the day, when Doc wasn't analyzing, he spent his time writing. He showed me many of his articles, but I don't remember any of them, except a new version of the Ten Commandments. I guess during his days as a professional analyst he found many patients suffering from guilt – a fact caused by their breaking one or other of the Commandments. So Doc's version of each Commandment was a little more lax than the original. For instance, the Seventh Commandment, which stated that Thou Shalt Not Covet Thy Neighbour's Wife, became Thou Shalt Not Make A Habit Of It. Therefore, it was really hard to break any of the Commandments, as Doc's version gave you a lot of leeway.

I don't recall ever seeing any of his works published, but he was always after his nephew John Fisher (Mr. Canada), to do something about having them presented to the world. The Fish always promised to try, but I guess he never got around to it. He did, however, leave Doc and me many a bottle of rum, and to this day I feel deeply indebted.

It was almost five years to the day that I first met Doc, when I returned to the house and Ruby told me he had succumbed to a heart attack, dying in the bathtub. So, like the departure of my friend Olga, the passing away of old Doc seemed to cast a spell on the house. Things were never the same.

Mrs. Campbell, the chiropractor, also suffered a heart attack. They took her away to a nursing home where she died a couple of months later. The next to succumb was Miss Hubble who, gloves and all, had picked up some virus. She, too, up and passed away at St. Joseph's hospital, down the street.

Ruby began slipping again, after the death of her two medical advisors. Soon, she was spending all her time in bed, with Laurie waiting on her hand and foot. Finally Laurie was called to go to Finland, to spend the last days with his invalid sister. Laurie had no more than arrived in Finland when one of Ruby's cousins – who seemed to take a lively interest in Ruby's rather sizeable bank accounts – had her placed in the Riverdale Hospital.

Well when Laurie returned from Finland to find Ruby gone, he was more than upset – which was unusual for him. He went to the hospital and demanded Ruby's immediate release. Ruby was all for it, too, but the doctors were of a different opinion. As a result, Ruby was never to return to her house in Indian Grove.

Laurie became the sole occupant of the first floor of the house, and I was the only inhabitant of the second. The attic was taken up by a mother coon, who each spring produced offspring of at least five. The house was quiet all day and most of the night, until about two in the morning, when the coons would begin performing. The noise in the attic would last till just before daybreak.

By this time, Laurie had given up entirely on the cooking. The odd time he ate, it was down at a tiny restaurant just a block away. It also became apparent that Ruby had been a little lax in one phase of her training. Laurie was never able to handle the heavy responsibility of paying the household bills. He was supposed to gather all the bills at the end of the month, and take them down to Ruby and have her make out a cheque in payment, but often it would be six months before he got around to it. Daily, after such a lapse of time, there'd be phone calls from the hydro, the water company, and Bell, for the unpaid bills. Laurie, always the gentleman, would field the calls, talking on about the weather or something else that might enter his mind; and the poor flabbergasted caller would give up almost in despair. Laurie would reply with his "God bless you," and we were never without heat, light, and a telephone – though there were times when we may have been mighty close. I generally listened to all of these conversations, and when I felt things were getting desperate, would gather up Laurie and the bills and head for the hospital.

After a year or so at Riverdale, Ruby became quite contented, as she claimed that all her old friends dropped in each day to see her. On each visit she would tell me how well Sam the Worm Picker, Maclean, Doc, and Mrs. Campbell looked, and what a pleasant visit she had just had with each one of them.

Yes, Ruby became quite contented, but Laurie began to slip rapidly. His memory was the first thing I noticed going. When he'd come to my room, he'd call me Jenny – the Irish Setter's name – or Deany, the budgie's name, and the budgie by my name. Well, neither the bird nor the dog seemed to care all that much, but when I checked him up on it he became a little vexed, and didn't come up to my room for a couple of nights. Finally, one night he made his way up, barely able to climb the steps, and collapsed on a chair in my room. He said, "Laurie is sick." Immediately I rushed him to the hospital. He was indeed sick, as right off they placed him in

Emergency – where he remained for five days with no visitors allowed. Finally, on the sixth day, Loop and I were able to visit him. We were walking by the nurses' station, when the Head Nurse collared us and asked if we were friends of Mr. Paauola. We said we were, and she wanted to know all the particulars. When we had filled her in she said in a stern professional manner, "You know it took us nearly three days to get him cleaned up." Pulling his spectacles down to the end of his nose the Loop, in his best courtroom manner, replied, "Now that you've gotten down to the skin, I hope you realize that you've found the finest fellow who ever walked."

It was just a matter of days when I received a call at two in the morning, informing me that Laurie the Butler had passed away peacefully. On entering the hospital ward, I was greeted by the same Head Nurse who, this time, had tears in her eyes. She told me that near the end she had asked him if he was suffering, and he replied with a beaming smile, "No, God bless you." The smile still hung on his face, although his eyes were closed, when I said my next-to-final farewell to the Butler, and they wheeled him away on a stretcher.

The public trustee handled everything. Laurie never looked better in life, as he lay in peace in the undertaker's parlour with a brand new suit – and the smile still there. Since nobody ever knew Laurie to practice any formal religion, I advised the undertaker that it might be wise to engage a Lutheran minister, because Laurie had once told me that he had attended a Lutheran church as a child.

The service was short – five minutes at the most – performed by a rather elderly minister, supporting himself with two canes, with only the Loop and me in attendance. As the two of us were about to make our departure, one of the attendants handed me the visitor's book, which now lies on my shelf. At the time it contained only two names: the Loop's and mine. But gradually I found myself filling the pages with the names of all those who would have wanted to be there: Ruby, Maclean, the Worm Picker, Olga – and the list goes on.

The day after the funeral I went to see Ruby to tell her about Laurie's passing, and of his burial here in Beachwood Cemetery. "You're drinking again!" she said, quite disgusted. "Why, he just left a minute or so before you arrived."

A few months later the call came from Riverdale to tell me Ruby had joined Laurie. They buried her down near Port Hope beside

Auntie. Her last years weren't at all bad, when you consider those daily visits she had with her friends. Yet, damn it all, old Jim, who, at ninety-three, had just been married for the fourth time, failed to show.

My stay at Indian Grove was at last coming to an end. It was just a matter of weeks before the Public Trustee stepped in again, and the house was sold to – of all people – the Jesuits. They planned to build a senior citizen's complex, and they promised there would be a place for me when I was ready for it. In the meantime, they provided me with a basement apartment, just a backyard away, in a house on Parkside Drive.

The basement here at Parkside is not unlike the one at Madison Avenue. It has just been vacated by an artist, and the weird paintings that adorn the walls bring back old memories. Lately, like Ruby, I have been sitting here waiting for my friends, the Worm Picker, Garner, Maclean, Doc, Honest Jack, and Laughing Louie to show up.

Somehow I have come to believe that the first to show will be Laurie the Butler and Olga the Artist. For I think it was the two of them that I learned to understand and love the best. As the Loop says, "Nobody can understand any better than me what it is to be a little dirty both inside and out." God Bless you.

Skid Row to Easy Street

The mid-seventies marked the beginning of bad times for many of us – particularly for my High Park friends. Thanks to MPP Frank Drea, the price of a bottle of fortified wine almost tripled in no time. It sure played hell with my welfare buddies.

It used to take them only an hour or so to "stem" for a jug, but as the recession set in, and the cost trippled, they were lucky if they could afford a bottle a week. Now I don't want you to get the idea that Frank is any worse than the rest of our politicians, but for a fellow who used to like the odd snort himself, he sure jiggered my friends.

I know there are some of you out there who think booze is a vice – or a luxury at best – but for many of my friends it is unquestionably a necessity. It's the only medication that seems to cure what ails them. Take the case of Arthur the Irishman. Arthur had been a High Park regular for years – quite pleased with his state in life – until Minister Drea ups the price of a bottle of steam to unaffordable heights. Arthur, better known to his High Park friends as "The Swivel," had a problem with his head when he ran out of medication. Right out of the blue, his noggin started turning continuously, ten degrees short of a full circle – and continued to twist back and forth, like a clothes dryer. Several years ago in Ireland he had his illness diagnosed by some of the finest medical men in Dublin. They all came up with the same cure. They informed Arthur that his problem required a daily dose from the vine.

Eventually, Arthur's head-turning began to get on everyone's nerves, so High Park Wally, the Squire of the Park, called a meeting of all the regulars, to see if something could be done about getting Arthur his daily medication. Everybody came, Norbert the Writer, Handstand Louie, The Polish Pilot, The Fool and Flymaker, Mushroom Stan, Eddie the Informer, The Deer Stalker, the Weasel, Streetcar Larry, and even Washroom Mary.

Wally opened the meeting by telling the members about the Swivel's plight, but it was unnecessary, since Arthur was sitting nearby on the park bench, in the midst of one of his worst days. His head was turning faster than a plane's propellor, and every once in awhile he would lift right off the bench like he was going to levitate! All agreed that something had to be done immediately, if Arthur was to remain earthbound. This being Welfare day, it was decided that everybody in attendance would contribute five dollars to the Swivel's medication fund. The money collected, and any forthcoming, was to be placed in trust with lawyer Loop Montgomery, whose office was just across the way. Loop agreed to set up the trust to provide Arthur with enough cash each day to purchase one bottle of relaxant.

The arrangement was not a complete solution for Arthur, as one bottle did not exactly bring his head to a full stop, but it did slow the gyrations enough to reduce his tendency to levitate, and keep him from bumping into things. Additionally, he never seemed quite as happy as in the old days, and sort of kept to himself, but otherwise acted normally – apart from a slight wobble.

The arrangement was even worse for the Loop however, because after the initial donations the only one donating to the cause was the Loop himself. But, by way of explanation, I think I should introduce you to Arthur's friends so you'll realize that life wasn't a bed of roses for them either.

I'll begin with High Park Wally, who was the leader of the pack. Wally came from a good family. There wasn't a day when he couldn't slip home for a change of clothes, a bite to eat, and a couple of bucks, providing his father happened to be out of the house. Wally once yielded to his childhood fantasies and became a railroader. Through some twist of fate – after he had served the company well for over ten years – he was found guilty of violating Rule G, which states that the use of any intoxicant is strictly prohibited while on railroad duty. To this day, Wally denies being guilty of such a shameful offence, and claims that it was not until years later (when he took on the heavy responsibilities of supervising the park), that he succumbed to the pressure, and took up drinking.

In stature alone, Wally had the appearance of a born leader. He was a tall, broad-shouldered fellow with a very engaging smile – the only regular member of the park who could be described as a lady's man. One rather chilly winter's evening when he and his friend the Weasel were wandering the park with no place to stay, they happened by chance to find the door to one of the ladies' washrooms ajar. On entering, they were confronted by the attendant, Washroom Mary. It was love at first sight. To seal the friendship, Mary gave Wally a pass-key, good for any washroom in the park. It was the beginning of better things for Wally and his friends, and each member was given a duplicate key, so that all were assured of a place to sleep when the weather was cold or disagreeable.

Now Norbert the German writer was cut from an entirely different block than Wally. He never forgot the fact that the Allies had won the war, and harboured a deep hatred for all the victorious countries – with Canada topping the list. He had the notion that since Canada was partly to blame for taking over his homeland, the least Canada could do was give him a free home, or at the very least a comfortable living.

On his arrival he was quite an accomplished writer, being able to write and converse in four languages. Many of the Canadian publications for which he wrote, found his contributions to have a distinctively Nazi slant. Needless to say, as a journalist he was not overly successful. Thus, he was forced to develop his second talent – that of being an accordionist. As a musician, he managed to play with several popular bands during the fifties and early sixties. Again however, his single-minded nature clashed with the majority viewpoint, and he was forced to go solo. For a time he managed to keep life and limb together by playing at the German and Austrian Clubs, but eventually he began to feel that his talents were not being appreciated enough. After only a fifteen-minute appearance in the stage he would seat himself at one of the tables and spend the rest of the evening sponging drinks. Suffice to say, he soon became *persona non grata* at the clubs. The end of his musical career marked the beginning of his revenge against the Canadian government – when he went on permanent welfare.

As for Handstand Louie, his background is something of a mystery. It's believed that he used to be a stunt man in Vienna, but the only stunts I ever saw him performing were standing on his head for hours at a time in the park, or walking on his hands. In the wintertime he always wore two pair of shoes – one pair for his feet, and a smaller pair for his hands. Now don't ask me to explain Louie's behaviour. His logic escapes me. I've watched him in his upside-down pose for hours at a time. It's known by the High Park regulars that he does come down the odd time – only for a moment or two, mind you – just long enough to gulp down a couple of slugs of wine.

High Park Wally says that Louie claims the world looks better to him upside-down. Additionally, he finds by remaining in such a position he only requires about a third of the alcohol normally needed for a glow. His reasoning being that all the alcohol in his blood remains in his head and thus cannot escape through his liver.

Mushroom Stan was always a loner, and kept to himself except when meetings were called. As the name implies, he picked and lived on mushrooms in season – freezing enough in a butcher store locker down on Roncesvalles to do him the rest of the year. He made mushroom soup, mushroom tea, had mushrooms fried and boiled, and even dried them in the warm summer sun and smoked them. Now Stan was the only member of Wally's gang who didn't drink, even though this was the major qualification to be a member. But if you ever smoked one of Mushroom's cigarettes you would know why he had been let in. One puff, and you're flying higher than the C.N. Tower.

Eddie The Informer, it is said, was once a cop and to this day he looks the part, powerfully built with a booming voice and an air of authority. He always managed to keep well-dressed, and even wore a tie. He was the only one of the group who never seemed to run short of money. But because of his background he was never given a full membership in the club, and Wally listed him as an associate member only. As a result, there were many little secrets that Eddy wasn't allowed to share. He was unaware, for instance, that the gang knew he was a paid informer of the Toronto police force. A lot of the information that Eddy got paid for – regarding the park in particular – wasn't too accurate. For you see, Eddy depended on the gang for most of his information, and the police depended on Eddy. As a matter of fact, Eddy was doing better when he worked the High Park district with Morality, knocking off the bootleggers. The cops would pay Eddy ten dollars to inform on local bootleggers, then give him another ten to go in and purchase a bottle. They would stand and wait for him to return with the evidence, but Eddy would always case the joint before a raid, making sure there was another exit, and would then disappear with the bottle. It was thus the Informer came to be demoted to park duty, much to the delight of the gang. They always made sure that when any offence was committed by a member of the club, somebody outside the gang was blamed.

The Deer Stalker and the Weasel were both old and quiet, and had seen better days. The Stalker would supply the odd goose or duck for our festive occasions. He would stalk them quietly at night. He was only caught once, when he decided that for a change he would procure a little venison. After slaughtering the deer, he dragged it to a house on McVity street where Mushroom had rented a room. As it was rather warm weather, he decided to get Mushroom to help him quarter it for storage in the butcher's locker. Investigating officers had no problem catching up with him, however, as they followed the trail of blood right to Mushroom's rooming house.

The Weasel was a little runt of a fellow, with tiny pointed ears and a black shiny beard that hung to his waist. He lived in a hole dug between two rocks at the highest point in the park, that was known to the boys as "Boot Hill." His only claim to fame was that he was infested by fleas. Whether because of his name or appearance, the fleas certainly enjoyed his company. They were his constant companions. Consequently, he was not even allowed to sleep in one of Mary's washrooms, and had to spend his nights in his little cave – all alone, except for Loop Montgomery's cat, Tramp. The cat would lie around Montgomery's office all day, scratching himself till late afternoon, when he would head up to the Weasel's abode.

Streetcar Larry was a cut above the others, because he was always clean and well-shaven, and dressed to kill. Somehow, he had given up on life a little – or at least enough that he didn't want to work anymore. Like Wally, who yearned to be a locomotive engineer, Larry had always wanted to be a streetcar conductor. He finally made it, but not for long. He was driving his car down Roncesvalles, where he was supposed to continue due south to King. When the car ahead of him stopped, the driver got out and threw the switch to head east along Dundas. For some reason or other Larry followed him. The passengers started screaming till finally someone pulled the emergency cord. After the car had come to a stop, a TTC Inspector appeared on the scene and relieved Streetcar of the only job he was ever to have.

As for Mary, well I never did get to know her all that well either, but like Arthur, she was born in Ireland, and upon her arrival in Canada had gone to work for the Parks Commission, looking after the lavatories. She did quite a commendable job, but there are some who say that she was doing more than just cleaning the toilets. I feel sure this is just idle gossip. All the gang liked Mary, especially after Wally had presented them with keys. Mary you see had big shifty eyes which would dart back and forth from side to side. But every once in a while they seemed to lock to the left – or the right. All the boys thought this kind of sexy, but it bothered Arthur. Whenever they met on one of the narrow paths in the Park they would collide, and the heated conversation that followed was always the same. Mary would say to Arthur, "Why don't you look where you're going?" and he would reply, "Why don't you go where you're looking?"

As for the Polish Pilot, and the Fool and Flymaker, I can tell you little about either of them, except that the Pole used to be a pilot in England with the Polish Resistance, and since coming to Canada had been flying rather high, without ever leaving the ground. The Fool and Flymaker was also Polish, and an accomplished tool and diemaker at one time, but decided he would rather sit, spit, and whittle than practice his trade. He fashioned fishing plugs and flys, but always seemed too tired to either fish himself or sell his wares.

Now that you know Arthur's friends, I think you can better understand the trust fund going short, and Montgomery having to foot the bill. Nevertheless, things were to change. One warm spring day around three months after the meeting about Arthur, I was sitting on a bench in the park, near the corner of Keele and Bloor, when up comes a cab and out jumps Arthur. He was all decked out in a new blue suit with all the trimmings. He walked toward me with the air of an aristocrat, head held high with nary a quiver. "I've got some sad news," he says, "Russian Joe died." That said, he pulled out a roll of bills big enough to choke a horse, and peeling off a twenty, tossed it at my feet. Then, rather nonchalantly said, "Buy yourself a cigar! I'm in a bit of a hurry to see my attorney, Mr. Montgomery."

Well, I had heard of Russian Joe. He was an elderly mustachioed old fellow, who rented rooms to the gang down on Marmaduke Street. Not that any of them ever stayed there very often, but they had to have an address for their welfare cheques. I sat for a long time wondering why old Joe's death could have such a miraculous effect on Arthur, and sort of finally passed it off as being like that old adage: one man's misfortune is another man's gain.

In a few minutes, I saw Arthur leave Montgomery's office, so more than a little curious, I stroll over to visit the Loop. I had barely gotten through the door when he said, "I've never in all my life seen such a changed man as that Arthur." Then opening Arthur's file, he showed me a pile of fiftys that Arthur had left for his fund. Next, the phone rang. It was the sergeant at 52 Division, to tell Montgomery that he's phoning on behalf of a client called Wally, who they picked up sleeping in the park, and were about to charge with vagrancy. However, the sergeant went on to say that when they were about to relieve him of his personal effects before putting him away, they were surprised to find he was carrying several thousand dollars in old George v bills. On questioning, Wally claimed that the bills were bequeathed to him by his Uncle Joe, who had just passed on.

Well, Montgomery told the sergeant he would be right up, and the two of us headed to the station, where Wally sat calmly waiting. Right off, the sergeant, who knew Montgomery said, "I wish you would tell your wealthy clients to get a room when they want to snooze," and he released High Park Wally in care of Mr. Montgomery – with no charge laid – and we headed back to the office.

It just so happened that Arthur's medication was laying on the desk, and knowing the Swivel would not be needing it that day, the Loop handed the bottle to Wally, who downed half in one gulp. Feeling a little better, he began to explain about the death of Russian Joe.

Through some twist of fate, all of the boys happened to be at the rooming house the day before, as the welfare cheques had all arrived.

When they had cashed the cheques and went to pay Joe for their mailing address, they found him in bed and in bad shape. Right off, they called a doctor and an ambulance, and rushed him to St. Joe's, down the street; but it was only a matter of hours till he passed away. His body was now resting at the hospital morgue, awaiting funeral arrangements.

Wally explained it was important that he get back down to the house and arrange for the burial. He asked Montgomery to come, so I tagged along, too. When we got there, the whole gang was in attendance, except for Eddy the Informer, who'd been sent to the east end on an important errand. I must say that nobody was looking all that sad, but nobody was smiling either. They all had kind of an undertaker expression on their faces. Right off, Wally said the meeting would be held in the cellar, so down we all went. Without mincing words, Wally said that he knew everybody had given the house quite a going over, and he was sure that all had come up with a little loot.

Getting on with it, Wally stated that it was certainly no business of his what each person had found, as it was a case of finders keepers. He went on to say that there might be those who believed the money belonged to Joe, but there was no proof, and as Joe had only owned the house for the past five years, it could have belonged to anybody. There was however one thing which had to be settled – that being the house. He said that he, personally, had given it a lot of consideration while up at the police station, and he would like to present the following proposal: "It is my opinion that each member should contribute the sum of one hundred dollars towards the cost of Joe's funeral. As Joe has no relatives or friends in Canada, by giving him a half decent burial there will be no questions asked. We can always scrape up enough to pay the taxes, and we'll all have a home for life."

Everyone agreed, except Norbert the German, who stated flatly that he was against it entirely. "I don't mind giving the odd dollar to the living, but I sure ain't contributing to the dead! Let the government bury him." Well this threw Wally's plan a little out of kilter, as it was a club rule that all members had to be in agreement before any important proposal could be passed. So Wally told Montgomery he would have to adjourn the meeting.

That evening Montgomery gets the word from Wally, so he contacts the Public Trustee and a couple of officers come up, search the joint, and put a padlock on all the doors.

Joe had a nice funeral with every member there, including Norbert, contributing two wreaths each. There were more flowers than mourners. Montgomery had I were both asked to act as pallbearers. He engaged a lawyer friend of his, named Hill, to help carry his side of the coffin, and I got a friend of mine to help with my side. After the funeral everybody headed for the Rondon Hotel, and an even sadder ceremony was held to mark the breaking up of the old gang.

The very next day Arthur was on a plane to Dublin – back to his homeland, where he felt sure he would never run short of medication. After a bit, the Weasel got shaved up, then shampooed in a car-wash down on Dupont Street, and to be on the safe side, had a flea collar made, which he wore around his neck for a couple of weeks. He now lives in a nice senior citizens' apartment not far from the park. His neighbour, just down the hall, is none other than the Flymaker, who couldn't be more contented. He has a little balcony where he spends hours, sitting, whittling, and spitting.

Washroom Mary, well she got a couple of nice print dresses out of the deal, as well as a big promotion. She is now washroom attendant at one of the larger hotels here in the city and often comes home with ten dollar tips – so maybe all that gossip wasn't too far out.

Wally comes to the park occasionally, but only to walk his dog. With all the responsibilities of running such a large organization off his shoulders, he has cut down considerably on his intake. He now resides at home with his parents, and things couldn't be going better.

Street Car Larry is back in his element, riding the street cars and the subway as a paid passenger from early morning till long after dusk. He has a lovely wife with a good job, who more than provides for them both.

Handstand Louie and the Polish Pilot both flew out of the country, two days after Arthur, to some warm place in Spain, as the Canadian winters were getting them down.

Eddy the Informer, well, Wally looked after him, too. He put him on the plane with Handstand and the Pilot – but it seems with a one-way ticket only. The odd time one of the boys gets a card from him asking for passage back, but to date all cards have gone unanswered.

Norbert the German was the only one who didn't change all that much. He still sits alone in the park writing his memoirs or playing his brand-new accordion. He has quit drinking wine altogether, and is gradually getting even with the government. He discovered a new brew called bitters which is supposed to be a tonic and, like groceries, isn't taxed. It's twice as potent as wine and is sold in every grocery and butcher shop in the Polish village. He had a charge account at two outlets, so he never runs short. At the present time he is a little perturbed by a Roncesvalles doctor, Morty Shulman, who in a recent newspaper column sort of blew the whistle on bitters, complaining about the number of empty bitters bottles cluttering the street in front of his office.

Now and again, Norbert will talk about the old days, but the only time a smile seems to cross his solemn face is at the mention of Russian Joe. His smile is in no way in disrespect of Joe, but a way of having another laugh at the Canadian government. For you see, he has been drawing his welfare cheque all these years, and all of Joe's worldly goods, including the old house on Marmaduke, went to the Russian government. All, that is, except his money – or *was* all that money Joe's?

My kind of people **15**

Old Memories Are Best

Here it is, the winter of '87, and I'm up at the Ontario Science Centre, running an old steam engine about to celebrate her 100th birthday.

Now before any of you liberated women get to raising hell about a steam engine being called "her," I want to put you straight. Yes! It is true that all ships and locomotives were always referred to as being feminine. This does not necessarily have to be attributed to the old adage, that anything under the direct control of man should be called "her." It goes deeper than that.

In spite of all this modern emancipation – men often get pretty confused about women. It's very seldom we know what to expect of them. And – I have to admit – it is the same way with steam-engines. Maybe they were just a bit smarter than we were – but they certainly knew what they wanted – and I never saw two that acted the same way.

Now take the 3100's, a class of locomotives, perhaps the most majestic engines ever built by the C.P.R. It is true that they only built two, but I guess two like that was enough! Like many beautiful women, they were fickle and not too dependable – although they were the most gorgeous girls that ever pulled a passenger train. Sometimes they would do what they were told, but more often they wouldn't – it all depended on whose company they were in. If they liked you, they would display their affection, doing anything asked of them. If they didn't, well that's another story.

But before I get to that, I should fill you in on their roots. Their names were "Dot" and "Daisy" – "3100" and "3101." They were born in Montreal, and fathered by a railway official – I forget his name – as I was never overly impressed by railway men who wore suits and ties. It seems he was more interested in siring an actress than an ordinary dependable housewife.

For some time, the twins pulled the fast passenger trains, "21" and "22," which ran at night from Montreal to Toronto. One would be on the eastbound train and the other would be going west. It is rumoured that there was a lot of jealousy between them, and that the 3101 could outrun the 3100. They would meet each night at Tichbourne – a desolate village, north of No. 7 Highway, and greet each other with two shorts on the whistle, a highball, meaning all is well with the world. They were in service some thirty years and finally retired to a more gracious life, displaying their graceful lines in two separate museums – Dot, the 3100, in Ottawa and Daisy, the 3101, in Calgary. Even today, they make it quite clear that they are there to be looked at and not touched.

Now I can tell you quite a few "Hoggers" from Smith's Falls who have had a close relationship with them both, and I guess their families would not mind. There were Si Deegan, George Suffel, Mike Merea, Frank White, Jack Beeth, and perhaps a dozen others. It is said that both girls liked a little variety. Yet even when they were young, they always went for older men, and thus they were less than courteous with any young engineer or fireman who happened to appear on the scene for the first time.

I guess I was a little lucky, as I was only called on once to fire old Daisy. I had gone to Trenton on a freight train and the regular fireman on "21" had taken sick. So, since I was the only man available, my old friend Bill Powell, the regular hogger, was stuck with me. He warned me, as we were sitting at Trenton station, that the old girl didn't take much to strangers. He also advised me to turn on the stoker, and using the front jets only, get a pile of coal up front beneath her arch. This was the opposite to what you did with any other stoker engine. He then went on to say that we would be pulling twenty coaches, so he would have to use her a bit,

Well, I was lucky to be with Bill, rather than a lot of the other hoggers who were on that run. He never seemed to get too excited and would sit back relaxed, puffing his pipe. At Belleville, I was short seventy-five pounds of steam, and I never got it back throughout the journey to the Falls. Bill would keep easing her off when he could, and worked her as gently as possible, with the quadrant almost on centre. Now and again he would break out in a smile and say, "Come on you old bastard, give the kid a break!"

Finally, we arrived in the Falls an hour late, and when the east-end crew took over and the train had left, we went into the station restaurant for a coffee. Now you may have noticed I stated that we had waited for the train to leave, and there was a reason for that. In those days, in every railway restaurant, there were two menus – both exactly the same – but the price list was different. The low price was for local people and the higher one for travellers or "foreignores," as they were called. I guess I was quiet, a little ashamed, when Billy finally broke the silence with the words, "I think the old bastard kind of took a liking to you but it's that time in the month when a lot of women get a little bitchy."

Now old "Sulky Sarah," the wheelock engine I am now running, is no majestic locomotive, as she spent most of her existence in a furniture factory in the west end of Toronto. Somehow, like me, she ended up in the scrap heap, where she was retrieved by the Centre and restored to her original splendour. No, Sarah did not live a glamorous life like the twins, travelling across the country. I suppose because of this she lacks culture. She was more of a drudge, working in the old factory and doing whatever was required of her. Don't get me wrong, however, she must have been glamorous once – as a matter of fact, she has aged well. That leads me to believe that she, too, must have had one special man in her life. Somehow I have come to believe that in her prime she was a one-man woman and, until his death, she was well looked after.

For any of you that have never heard of a "wheelock" steam engine, they were born in Galt in the late 1800's, and when they came of age, they went to work in various industries throughout Ontario. There was quite a big family of them – I am not quite sure how many. Some worked in sawmills, others went to generating plants, and many, like Sarah, went to work in various factories throughout the province.

Indeed, Sarah is no majestic locomotive, with black smoke bellowing from her stack, she is too much of a lady to be seen smoking. There is no steaming water sputtering from open cylinder cocks, a moaning air pump, or panting dynamo. She does not even smell like a locomotive – that mixture of hot oil and coal. When you open the throttle there are no rods to churn the drivers, steel against steel, with sparks flying, until the sanders to do the job, and help the locomotive stay on its feet. You can't see her digging like the old hogs did, barking furiously as they lifted their train, with the barks gradually becoming softer as you hooked them up, and the voice from the exhaust became almost a mumble, uttering rapidly, as the puffs become shorter, the words, "I got her beat, I got her beat, I got her beat." No, there is none of that, but Sarah, in her retirement, lets you blow the whistle – unlike Dot and Daisy – and the kids come running from every direction, shouting, "Is that a "Choo Choo" Mister?"

Well, I have to explain it is not a locomotive, but it works on the same principal, and so you try to explain to the older children how a steam engine works.

There is never a day that some old railroader "don't happen by" – many I have known, or heard of. This one particular morning, I had just awakened old Sarah by gradually opening her throttle. She was moaning and groaning and coughing a bit, before she decided to begin her day. I looked around and who's standing watching me but my old railway buddy, "Puddin'."

"Heard you were up here!" was his greeting. "I was taking a walk in the park and the door was ajar, and I thought I would pay you a visit. Besides, I'm taking up a little collection. Our friend "Stupe" just died down in Nashville, and the boys are chipping in to get his body back to town." Well, sad as I found the news, I had to smile, and I asked what the hell was Stupe doing down in Nashville, Tennessee. But when Puddin' added "Don't you see, he finally made it!," right away I understood, and I began thinking back a few years. But I'll tell you about Stupe in a minute.

First of all, I'd like to introduce you to Puddin'. Now, you've got to see "Puddin'" to understand how he got the nickname.

He's as wide as he is tall, and at one time he was supposed to be able to lift the wheels and the axle of a boxcar without help. He worked for years as a car-man down in the John Street yard, here in Toronto, and was always promoting some scheme or other to raise a little extra beer money. He has, what you would call, a long white beard if it hung on anybody else, as it more than covers his belly.

He was the only man whom I ever saw who could drink out of two quart bottles of beer at the same time. However, a man must do a lot more than this to become famous on the railway, and it was his ability as a fund-raiser that later became his trademark. If there was a death, Puddin' would be the first around in the morning to take up a collection for flowers. A wedding or sickness was never forgotten, and his collections for charity were unending – that is, if all the money went where it was intended. I suppose there will always be those skeptics that thought a lot of it went in the Puddin's pocket. Some of it did, the Puddin' now maintains, but only that which was required for expenses.

So it was through Puddin's fund-raising that I first heard tell of the "Stupe," which some of the more ignorant fellows around said meant "short and stupid." All the boys down at John Street thought the world of the Stupe. He would come to work every morning dressed in his cowboy makeup – Stetson, pointed boots, chaps, and he always brought his guitar.

It was feared for a while that the gang might lose their entertainer when he was sent, mistakenly, by a new foreman, to Union Station to check on the well-being of the Chicago Flyer before she pulled out. It was the car-man's job to check all the journals on the coaches, and make sure that none of them were running hot. They would then get to the engine, where they would give the sideroads of the engine a little tap with the hammer, to see there were no cracks. Of course, a good man is able to tell by the sound of the ring from the blow. Well, the Stupe was performing his duties, and when he came to the engine, he started tapping the rods when, just then, up walks a new official. "Why do you hit those rods with your hammer?," he asked, not knowing himself. "I'll be goddamned if I know," replied the Stupe, "but I've been doing it for thirty years."

After that encounter, it was deemed best by the car foreman that he should stay away from the station. So, he was given a vacant section-man's shack, and became a full-time entertainer for the gang. Now I'm not quite sure if the "brass" ever knew that they had an entertainer on the payroll, not that it mattered that much, as the rest of the boys were more than glad to pitch in and take up any slack.

Don't get me wrong, the Stupe was no "shirker." He took his job seriously, and no matter who came to the shack, he gave them a performance worth remembering.

Anyhow, one year the Puddin' was having a rather slack time. Nobody died, nobody got married and only one fellow was pensioned (that being Stupe himself). So Puddin' figures that since, he too, was going to be pensioned in a month or so, he should undertake one more act of charity. The next pay day he was out canvassing for his friend the Stupe. He made the rounds – the freight sheds, the roundhouse, shops, ice-house, and all the hotels frequented by the boys in those days – Walker House, Barclay, and the Lambton. The "canvas" lasted over a week. Now anyone who knows railroaders understands they never refuse to donate to a good cause, when it comes to a fellow-employee. So, the Puddin' had the Stupe come along with him, dressed up in brand new regalia (his own donation).

Puddin' explained to all that he had received a letter from Johnny Cash's agent, and they wanted Stupe down in Nashville right away.

The day they set for their departure was to be a day after the Puddin' was to be pensioned. He felt he should wait around for anything coming his way, as he had been so generous with so many others. However, since the collection was quite a lot bigger than he had bargained for, he decided that he should get Stupe a new guitar, as the one he had had gone too many miles. Thus, he took him down to McTamney's Pawn Shop on Sherbourne Street, and got him a dandy.

That night, when he and the Stupe parted, everything was in order. They would leave the next morning on the "Flyer." Stupe was to meet Puddin' at Gate 4.

Well, that night, it is said that Puddin' lost his favourite sister. He left right away for the Emerald Island. He did, however, manage to leave a message with the stationmaster to head off Stupe, and tell him why the trip had been cancelled. Some say the Stupe took it pretty hard when he appeared in his best and was given the sad news, but he sort of passed it off with the words, "Well, at least I got me a brand new outfit, and I will be all set when Puddin' gets back." To the best of my knowledge, the Puddin' was unfortunately gone for a long time, and when he turned up at the Science Centre it was the first I'd seen of him in several years.

As you can see, I was more than interested in how the hell the Stupe had managed to pass away in Nashville, Tennessee. So the Puddin' fills me in. It seems that the Stupe had a daughter who had married quite well, down in that State, and knowing her father's love for country music, she had invited him there for the winter, where he unfortunately succumbed. So here it is, some twenty years later, and the Puddin' has showed up for what could well be his last job of fund-raising and who could be a better recipient than his old friend, the Stupe? I asked him what all the boys were donating and he said "Only a buck." "You know," he went on, "the Stupe had so many friends. I can raise the shipping fee easy, and I wouldn't want to have anything left over. I wouldn't feel right." Well, just to be on the safe side, I handed him a deuce, in case he changed his mind and took his regular commission.

Thanking me ever so kindly, he was about to leave when I told him he should wait around as I was expecting my partner, "Westinghouse" Benny Barrett, another old railroader, who works with me at the Centre. I had no more than got the words out of my mouth, when who should come along but Benny and two other railway pensioners – "Highball" Jack and "Golden Arm" Atkinson.

They were both surprised as hell when they see Puddin' because, like me, they thought he had passed away. Well, Puddin' tells the boys the sad news and they make their donation. It was then felt that since we were all together, maybe for the last time, we should have a little visit.

"Highball" asked Puddin' if he ever sees his old friend "Sleep-Out" Louie, and Puddin' informed him that "Sleep-Out" is dead, but his wife, "Half Moon," is still alive and living back on the Reserve near Deseronto.

Now, "Sleep-Out" and "Half Moon" were a story in themselves, and some of the stories get a little racey so Benny says, "Maybe we should go up behind the boiler to stop any of the public from listening in." Once we're there, Highball began with the time Louie got married. The night before the ceremony, Sleep-Out had gone up to stay close by Half-Moon's shack. He took a few presents with him, including a new pair of shoes. It was winter-time, with a lot of snow on the ground and the next day, when they left the house, there was Half Moon, wearing her first pair of high heels. As they approached his car, "Sleepy" noticed that his bride-to-be was walking backwards, which he found rather strange. "Why are you walking that way?" he asked. "Because I like to see my tracks in the snow," was her reply.

Everyone recreates his own concept of the past. Automation quickly shifts the course of history, so that the living images which helped shape that past are swept by the electronic winds of modern times.

So it is with the old "iron horse." Perhaps no other image presents such a sharp, clear picture of a vanished people and changing times as the steam locomotive. Few remember the ancient "Hogs," plagued with the dry heaves, huffing, puffing, and crying defiantly, "I own the track, so stand well back."

Oh, there are still a few left, such as the one in Ottawa – a real ghost I guess, for railroad buffs. Old 1201 makes a twice-weekly excursion from Ottawa to Wakefield, Quebec. Although I never like to see the last of anything, I went down to see her in Ottawa. As I stood watching the crew dismount, I suddenly became overcome with loneliness.

I climbed up into the fireman's seat and looked across to the hogger's side. It was then I realized that I was not alone. Mysteriously, I found myself back in the past, and one-by-one my old friends appeared.

There was C.J. with his southern drawl, "Whiskey Jack," the "Montreal Chinaman," "Rubber Belly," "Preacher Lange," "Driver Gibbey," and "Rulebook Ike," "Cold Water," "Powder Puff" – and still they came.

No, it was not the lonesome call of a steam whistle that had brought me back to my home in the Valley this dismal, cloudy day. It was something deeper.

I had not come to pay homage to a great monument of the past, the ultimate in mechanical splendour, I had come to revisit the spirit that drove her. Unlike the admiring railroad buffs, who idolize the image, I knew the secrets from within.

I had fired old 1201 hundreds of times, along with her sisters of the twelve hundred series. They were all show! I never knew one that could pull its designed tonnage, or stay on its feet on a steep grade.

They had an exhaust steam injector which couldn't supply water to a tea kettle. I could go on and on, but what's the use. The Preacher said it best: "It takes a good pilot to fly a bad plane."

Let the Sunday excursioners romanticize what they may, I prefer the reality – memories of friends: real friends; and of men: real men. They were a breed apart – rough and tough – but men of principle. They saw it all. They kept their eyes open, unless turning a blind eye was more prudent. Oh, they had their trials and tribulations too, like the crews of the Almonte wreck, who had faced death, and perhaps worse, through a lifetime of accusations.

The men of the road sing a different song than the one sung in the Valley hotels, and immortalized by Mac Beattie. Even the tune is different. I guess the boys wouldn't mind if I gave you part of one little verse:

> At Pakenham they asked for time,
> As they knew the eighteen wasn't steaming.
> The request was denied
> And thirty-seven died,
> The night of the Almonte wreck.

There is a lot more to that song, but it is not for publication. It might point an accusing finger, and the boys wouldn't want that. Jack Howard, in his farewell note to his son, said it all, "Let God be my judge, I broke no rules." I know he was speaking for all the crew members involved. If there are any trains up in the great beyond, I know Jack, and his Hogger on that fateful night, will be riding first class. I wouldn't be too surprised if the old Hogger, Bill Richardson, who spent his last days working as a bitter, broken man on the end of a shovel in the Prescott yard, will have his own private car. He paid his dues.

Let's close the books on the Almonte wreck, for now at least. It's better for all that we not even sing the song, its refrain is good enough:

> No it wasn't the teaming,
> But an engine not steaming
> That was the cause of the Almonte wreck.

But wait, I hadn't come home again to judge and criticize. Let the old steamers have their place in history. I enjoy Mac Beattie and his songs – especially when winter sets in and the wind is from the north. The railroad buffs are surely entitled to the monuments of the past. Yet I had returned for something different – memories: pleasant memories of my kind of men, some long gone.

What better place for a laugh than to be back in time with the boys.

To again hear "Rule Book Ike," holding court in a snow-bound bunkhouse in Chalk River. The meeting being interrupted by a visiting official asking, "What are you complaining about today Mr. Schofield?" "About a cheap outfit that makes its men work ten years for a pass," was the reply. "If you were working for a farmer, would you expect him to drive you home?" the Brass interjected. "You're damn right boy, if he was going my way."

Isn't that "Cold Water," dozing over in the corner of the cab? Here is a man who was years ahead when it came to conversation. He never built up 250 lbs. of steam when 150 would get him over the road. There's "Whiskey Jack," with his goose-necked oil can, and a hunk of waste for wiping up spills, climbing down to oil the big ends. There, too, is the Master Mechanic, berating Jack for his past sins. Jack keeps nodding his head in agreement, with the can aimed at the official's new trousers. I can still hear the shouting as he gave the throttle an extra nick and headed north.

"Whiskey" was not all bad. It's said that when he finally discovered the life of sobriety, he had gathered many converts along the way. He did, however, have one failure in that line, too. This was a fellow named "Blades" Code. Blades' lifetime lament was that he had not been enshrined in the Hockey Hall of Fame, due to the fact that he had endorsed beer, rather than Bee Hive Syrup.

Anyway, Jack's attempt at converting Blades occurred one day on the steps of the Lee Hotel. Jack asked, for an opener, if Blades had found God. "Didn't know he was lost," was the curt reply, as the "great" hockey player disappeared behind the beverage room door.

As I continue to remember the past, I see the "Driver" is here, too, and he's waving at a farmer in a ploughed field near Cobden. "Who's that you're waving at?" someone asks. "Ain't sure. He waved at me and I wove at him and I knewed I knowed him." Maybe his English wouldn't be accepted by today's scholars, but it had to be better than the language of the "Montreal Chinaman." The Chinaman was something else. He was short, stout, with a blown-up, tomato face, a foaming mouth, and lips that were always moving. What he was saying, I will never know, but his French was even worse. Thus his name, the "Montreal Chinaman."

"Rubber Belly," who has also just appeared, disputes that claim, and he should know. He grew up with the Chinaman in Griffon Town, and socialized with him all his life. The moniker, the fat man claims, was hung on the Chinaman during the races at old Blue Bonnets. It seems that after a bad month at the track, the big one turned to his betting adviser, informing him in no uncertain terms that, "You couldn't pick your brother out of a room full of Chinamen." "So take your pick."

The other Griffen Towner was just plain "Frenchy," and had no trouble conversing in either language, although he never wore his teeth. For some reason or other, he always carried them in the bib of his overalls, beside his Hamilton watch. He was pulling light one night, with only the engine and the caboose, when he suddenly came upon a flagman at the top of Hailey Hill. Somehow the brakes failed, and he ran out of track, as the section men had been changing a rail at the foot of the grade. For some, I suppose the experience might have been a bit frightening. But the crew managed to jump to safety on one side of the track, while the engine lay, moaning and groaning on the other. Pointing at the engine, Frenchy nonchalantly warned his friends, "You better stand back boys, she's trying to get up."

And isn't that Arthur Doyle, rounding a curve at Sand Point with the engine swaying and dipping? When it finally rights itself, he proclaimed, "It's a hell of a great thing we don't have to steer 'em."

C.J. has just taken over the throttle, so maybe its time for me to disembark. I know when Clifford leaves the yard he'll turn to the fireman with the request that he wave to his wife. She'll be standing behind their little house by the tracks, on the fireman's side. So he'll give two toots – a highball – and when he takes up the slack and gets her rolling, he'll then proclaim with a smile, "Annie my dear, you're on your own."

I climb down the steel ladder, as I have one more call to make before leaving the Valley – the office – better known as the Lee Hotel, some forty miles away in Smiths Falls.

When I reach the Falls, I take a hidden side-road down behind the round house, where the coal chutes used to stand. This was the home of my friend, Tom Penman. Yes, you guessed it, one of the descendants and heirs I am told, of that great lingerie company. Tom spent his years hidden away from the company's fortune, shovelling coal in the old chutes. His only failing in life was that he refused to cash his pay cheques, which made it a little hard on the company accountants. Come to think of it, he wasn't much of an advertisement for Penmans either, as he never wore underwear.

Then I drove down to the end of the lane, to the shack of my drinking buddy, "Ham the Rat." "Ham" was a busy man, as he had two jobs, imbibing, and raising white mice. His only problem was, that being a bachelor, he was unable to leave his abode without taking his mice along. So he had coveralls especially designed by "Scoop Penman," with three extra pockets, which allowed him to take his tiny friends along when he wanted to socialize. He would feed them draft from an eye-dropper when the waiters weren't looking.

After that visit, I crossed the tracks and entered the Knotty Lee Hotel. I walked over to the head table, which was vacant, and ordered a gingerale. I felt a little sad at first, looking around and not recognizing anyone, until my eyes fell on a picture hanging on the wall. It was a picture of these two genuine teetotallers, old Knotty, and his baseball buddy, Connie Mack. It seemed as if it was only yesterday that I had sat one table down from that picture, with my friend, "Barber Bill." A group of American vacationers had come in and seated themselves beneath the portrait. Since Knotty was there in person that day, they wanted to get acquainted with this living baseball legend. So they called him over to their table. To begin the conversation, one of them asked Knotty his opinion on the best brand of Canadian beer. "None of it's any good," was the blunt reply. "A pig wouldn't drink it." "What's more," he added, "my friend Mr. Mack wouldn't appreciate a beer stuck under his nose." It was not the American visitors that Knotty was really addressing that day, but Bill and me. He knew, in his sober wisdom, that drink had its place in life for those who could handle it. But he was against people indulging who couldn't. A few minutes later, he came to our table and informed us that we were cut off, and it was time we got back to work and on to better things.

Yet Knotty, in his wisdom, did not always have the final say. A week later, when Bill opened his barber shop, it was business as usual. There was a lineup of railroaders who had patiently awaited the "Barber's" return. Knotty was number nine in the lineup, and I brought up the rear. After what seemed like hours, Knotty finally plunked himself wearily into the barber chair. "What the hell do you want," old Bill shouted, and with the wave of his thumb like an umpire calling a third strike, added "Get out, you're cut off!"

Yet maybe I should take that statement back about Knotty not having the final say. Bill was to overcome the "Irish Plague," and lived a long and productive life, and I've been a gingerale drinker for years. No wonder Knotty seems to be smiling in that picture – something unusual for him.

For a while I sat on in the Lee Hotel, hoping some of the old survivors would come in. Time has a way of playing tricks, however, so I decided it was best to leave. I wanted to remember the boys the way they were, and twenty-five years is a long, long time.

I climbed into my car and began my exit from the Valley. I passed Clifford's little house by the tracks, and sounded two toots on my horn, as a salute to him and Annie. I drove down Beckwith Street, past the old town hall made famous by His Worship, "Daddy Marks," a former mayor. This hall was his monument, as his little office there was his home, and the battered old desk in the corner served as his bed. I sounded one little toot, for he, too, was my kind of man. (A two-toot salute from me is reserved for the men of the road.)

I reached Belleville before I realized I was pulling light. I had left part of me behind in the Valley, but most of it in Kingston: my heart. Yet I knew as I drove along that that's where it belonged. I was pulling all the tonnage I needed, a boxcar filled with memories. Who says you can't go home again?